Espionage

Michael Tregenza

Hamlyn

London · New York · Sydney · Toronto

FOREWORD

A great deal has been written recently about the exploits of Intelligence agents in various countries but little is known of the secret government agencies and departments which control and direct the hidden armies of spies. Everyone has heard of the CIA and KGB, the largest and most publicized of all Intelligence agencies, but not so well-known are the many other secret departments around the world such as the East German HVA, Polish Z-2 and Egyptian GIA. This book attempts to penetrate the hidden world of espionage and describe the organization and activities of the main Intelligence departments which operate on a world-wide scale and the men who direct the agents. In certain cases it has not been possible or advisable to give detailed information about methods of operation or the exact location of certain departments for the inevitable reasons of security.

My thanks are due to several people who have contributed information and assistance during the preparation of this book, in particular Pamela Taylor who typed the manuscript, Diana Condell and Laurie Milner who kindly loaned me certain equipment used by British and Polish agents, and the staff of Radio Free Europe in Munich and London who provided far more information than I could possibly use here.

I should also like to thank those sources in Warsaw, Berlin and London who willingly or unwittingly made useful contributions to this book.

M.T.

Published by the Hamlyn Publishing Group Limited
London · New York · Sydney · Toronto
Astronaut House, Feltham, Middlesex, England
Copyright © The Hamlyn Publishing Group Limited 1974
ISBN 0 600 33085 0
Phototypeset by Filmtype Services Ltd., Scarborough
Colour separations by Colour Workshop Ltd., Hertfordshire
Printed in Spain by Mateu Cromo, Madrid

CONTENTS

GREAT BRITAIN

Intelligence Service

During recent years the true nature of Intelligence Services and their functions has been successfully obscured and deliberately distorted by the revelations of a wide variety of defectors, double agents, sensation-seeking journalists, and occasionally by Governments. Basically, the role of a peacetime Intelligence Service is to keep the Government as well-informed and up to date as possible about the objective realities of the world in which it operates and to which its various policies must be related. A Secret Service therefore makes organized attempts at forecasting over a wide range of subjects, not only military and political, but also economic and social. It is obvious, therefore, that espionage in one form or another must necessarily be one of the most important activities of any Government, and the most secret.

(Below right) Sir Stewart Menzies, head of MI6 during World War I; *(below left)* Sir John Rennie, director of British Intelligence who retired in June 1973.

Former headquarters of British Intelligence at 21 Queen Anne's Gate, St James's, London SW1 which backs on to Broadway Buildings opposite St James's Park underground station. Inside they are in fact one large building. They have undergone extensive rebuilding, the Intelligence Service having moved to a new twenty storey office block in South London not far from Waterloo station.

Secrecy certainly exists in Great Britain where details of British Intelligence have, until recently, been kept out of public reach, in spite of the fact that abroad such details are often well-known and occasionally printed. For example, the name of the head of DI6 – Britain's Secret Service – and details of his career have never been officially announced and he usually remains unknown to the majority of the public. Such information has always been restricted with the aid of a set of documents called D-Notices. These have been issued from time to time by the Defence, Press and Broadcasting Committee and request the recipient not to publish certain sensitive information in the interests of national security.

However, early in 1973, a report appeared in a West German magazine naming the head of DI6 as Sir John Rennie, and shortly afterwards his photograph appeared in the British press with brief details of his career. It was said that Sir John had been appointed head of British Intelligence in the early 1960s, supposedly to bring the Service more directly under the control of the Foreign Office as he had previously had several years experience as a diplomat. Later in the same year reports appeared in the foreign press that a new Secret Service chief had taken over the running of British Intelligence. He was named as Mr Maurice Oldfield, a portly, bespectacled batchelor of 57 and a career Intelligence officer. Neither of these reports, although repeated in the British Press, was officially confirmed or denied.

The headquarters of DI6 (formerly MI6) was for many years located at 21 Queen Anne's Gate, St. James's, which backed on to and was part of 54 Broadway, opposite St. James's underground station. The Broadway section, however, was innocently labelled as a sub-branch of the Ministry of Land and Natural Resources; a Ministry which has not existed for several years. A telephone call to the Queen Anne's Gate address now reveals that it is a spare line, DI6 having moved elsewhere.

Across the river Thames in South London, there is a large, 20-storey glass and concrete skyscraper with a petrol-filling station in the fore-court. On the ground-floor there are steel bars behind the plate-glass windows on either side of the main entrance. This is now believed to be the present headquarters of British Intelligence. Little else is generally known about DI6; certainly its activities and operations are hidden behind an impenetrable wall of official secrecy.

Even so, a small glimpse of British Intelligence at work is sometimes revealed, usually in the foreign press, especially in Eastern Europe. In 1967 British agents operating under diplomatic cover in Warsaw made contact with a civilian radio telegraphist, 28-year-old Adam Henryk Kaczmarczyk,

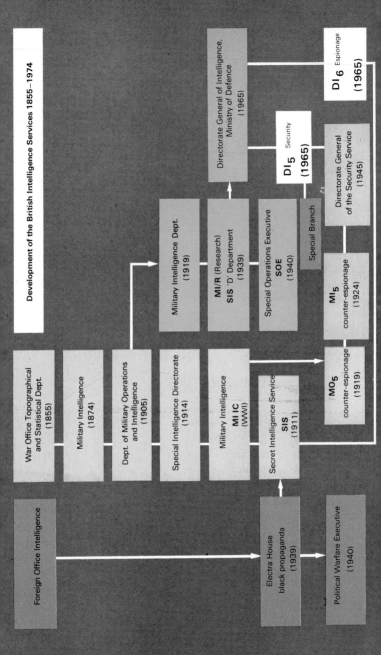

Development of the British Intelligence Services 1855-1974

War Office Topographical and Statistical Dept. (1855)

Military Intelligence (1874)

Dept. of Military Operations and Intelligence (1905)

Special Intelligence Directorate (1914)

Military Intelligence MI IC (WWI)

Secret Intelligence Service SIS (1911)

Military Intelligence Dept. (1919)

MI/R (Research) SIS 'D' Department (1939)

Special Operations Executive SOE (1940)

Directorate General of Intelligence, Ministry of Defence (1965)

DI₅ Security (1965)

DI₆ Espionage (1965)

Special Branch

Directorate General of the Security Service (1945)

MI₅ counter-espionage (1924)

MO₅ counter-espionage (1919)

Foreign Office Intelligence

Electra House black propaganda (1939)

Political Warfare Executive (1940)

(Left) 'Kim' Philby, double-agent. Became the head of an Intelligence department concerned with espionage and counter-espionage against the Soviet Union and was even tipped to become the director of MI6 at one time. Defected to the Soviet Union in 1963. *(Right)* German 'E'-boat of the type used to land British and West German agents on the Baltic coast of Poland and Russia from 1949 until 1955. The operation was unsuccessful owing to Philby's treachery.

who was employed at the time at an unspecified Polish military establishment.

Clandestine meetings were arranged between the Pole and three British agents at specially adapted flats in Warsaw occupied by British Embassy employees. The signal that it was safe to enter was a small Union Jack on the door. Inside, the flat was heavily curtained to deaden sound, and to further foil any bugging devices planted by Polish Security, loud music was always played; the conversations, during which information was passed, were conducted through an instrument resembling a doctor's stethoscope. During these meet-

ings, Kaczmarczyk provided the agents with information about the organization of communications in the Polish Army, the location of military objects and units, their organization, armaments and commanders, as well as information regarding the Polish Army's moral and political status during the Arab/Israeli Six-Day War of June, 1967.

Kaczmarczyk was eventually tracked down and arrested in a Warsaw restaurant by Polish military counter-intelligence men. At the same time the three British agents, a man and two women, were picked up and detained in one of Warsaw's main streets. The inevitable search revealed that one of the women's handbags contained several secret documents, sketches and reports obviously intended for British Intelligence.

Diplomatic immunity secured a quick release and hasty departure for London for the three agents. The Pole, however, was not so fortunate. After a four-day trial before a Warsaw district military court, conducted behind closed doors, he was sentenced to death and duly executed.

British's second Intelligence-gathering department, the Directorate-General of Intelligence, is not so secret as DI6, being mainly engaged in overt activities and openly run from the main Ministry of Defence building in Whitehall by Sir Louis Le Bailly, an expert on the Soviet Navy, and former Deputy Chief of Intelligence.

This department was formed in 1964 in an attempt to consolidate the three armed services Intelligence sections under one roof with one Director-General, thus eliminating the inter-service rivalry which had inevitably existed before; the merger was consolidated even further a year later when the service Intelligence directorates were abolished altogether and replaced by two bodies, the Directorate of Service Intelligence

Former headquarters of Section Five of British Intelligence at Prae Wood, St Albans, Hertfordshire. Section Five was concerned with counter-espionage and included the Iberian department, Five(d), directed at one time by Philby.

(DSI), and Management and Support Intelligence (DMSI).

The cost of running British Intelligence during 1973–74 is expected to be in the region of £15,000,000, according to the Supply Estimates. Although this figure is certainly far below what is actually spent it is the only one ever made public, and the Government is not obliged to provide any further details. Compared with previous Intelligence expenditure, this figure is £2,000,000 more than the previous year. No doubt the extra cost is due to the devaluation of the pound and an increase in Intelligence activities in Ireland. It is of course miniscule compared with the vast sums spent on Intelligence activities in the USA and USSR.

The British Intelligence building in Ryder Street, St James's, London, where Philby was employed as the head of Section IX, the anti-Soviet counter-Intelligence department.

Security Service

In any country the basic function of the State Security Service is the safeguarding of all information in the possession of the relevant government which, if disclosed to unauthorised persons would be likely to damage the interests of the country.

British Security, officially designated as the Directorate-General of the Security Service, or DI5 (formerly MI5), has its headquarters in a large, anonymous, white and red brick building in the heart of London's West End not far from the London Hilton. Here, the agents of DI5 quietly carry out their work of counter-espionage against the agents of foreign powers at work in Great Britain, especially those from Eastern Europe.

The directors of this anonymous secret security service are as faceless as the agents they control, their names completely unknown to the British public; DI5 itself does not officially exist, it is neither established by law nor recognized by Common Law. Needless to say, the methods and devices used are kept secret, although the more widely-used ones have become known such as the surveillance of those suspected of being foreign agents, especially diplomats of various nationalities who operate under diplomatic cover.

A standard method of surveillance which always causes a storm of public outrage whenever it is mentioned, is the interception of communications, ranging from the straight-forward opening of letters and tapping of telephones to the vetting and photocopying of cables and telegrams being sent to or received from abroad. This has been a standard security procedure in Great Britain for many years, but when brought to the attention of the public, usually via the Press, it never fails to arouse indignant comments about 'police state methods.' Officially, any such interception by DI5 may be carried out only on the authority of a warrant issued by the Home Secretary (the Security Service being answerable in a rather

Vernon Kell, first director of MI5. Between 1909 (when MI5 was first formed) and 1914 the staff consisted of Kell, four officers, three detectives and seven clerks. In spite of this almost total lack of staff for such an important department he scored some notable successes and proved the worth of his section as an effective counter-espionage force.

vague way to that government minister). Each application for such a warrant is carefully examined by the Home Office before a warrant is issued.

Occasionally the veil of secrecy may be raised a little to afford a brief glimpse of the inside of DI5; in 1961 for example, Gordon Lonsdale, the Soviet spy, pleaded not guilty at his trial thereby forcing the prosecution to reveal in court all they knew about the case, including the methods used by DI5 to detect and uncover his activities. All this had to be explained in detail in order to secure a conviction.

From its very beginnings in 1909 British Security had a tradition of always having a Service chief but this ended in May 1946 when Sir Percy Sillitoe became the first civilian head of DI5. Since then all its directors, including the present one, have come from civilian backgrounds. Sir Percy gathered around him a highly professional team of counter-espionage officers and agents dedicated to their work, Sir Percy himself, unlike all Security chiefs before and after him, making no secret of the nature of his profession. For many years he steadfastly refused to travel anywhere incognito or make use of cover identities.

The last director of DI5 to become known to the public was Sir Martin Furnival-Jones who retired from the post in 1972. Before doing so he testified to the Franks Committee, which was investigating certain aspects of the Official Secrets Act, on matters of national security.

During his appearance he was not identified by name, only by his official title of Director-General of the Security Service, usually abbreviated to DG-SS. Those present at the hearing were requested to keep his identity to themselves should they recognize the Director-General.

Sir Martin had been a career security man and directed DI5 for seven years during which time he restricted his interest in spies to the real thing; he made it known after his retirement that he never read any book relating to the subject with which he spent his working hours. Unlike Sir Percy he valued and enjoyed his anonymity, maintaining that in this way he was not restricted by a 'public image' which may well have affected the methods of operation used. The total lack of publicity therefore prevented any standards being set which would have to be lived-up to by his agents and successors as well as by himself.

DI5 has no powers of arrest, it can only carry out investigations; therefore when a case reaches the point where an arrest is the obvious end result, the security agents call-in the Special Branch which carries out the search of premises and the actual arrest.

Special Branch

A great deal of the effectiveness of DI5 depends upon the close co-operation of the Special Branch of the Metropolitan Police which acts as the executive arm of the Security Service.

Based at New Scotland Yard the SB employs between three and four hundred men in and around London with smaller

Sir Percy Sillitoe, director of British Security in the immediate post-war years.

sections in the provinces, notably at main air and sea ports. The officers of this department prepare prosecutions for DI5, using clandestine methods of investigation, although the use of electronic surveillance devices is probably not as common as is generally believed, as such methods are often expensive to maintain in terms of both money and man-power. This is certainly the case with telephone-tapping where the monitoring board has to be manned continuously day and night, a procedure which, if carried-out for any length of time, would necessitate employing a team of up to twenty men working in shifts. The total cost of such an operation is rarely justified by the end result. The type of person most likely to warrant the attentions of either DI5 or the SB is not going to divulge anything worth knowing on the telephone anyway. It is far easier to arrange with the GPO to have the line in question temporarily put out of action, thus effectively curtailing the activities of the suspect and reducing the amount of surveillance necessary.

Surveillance of one kind or another forms a large part of SB work, particularly the surveillance of foreigners. Each foreign community in Great Britain has its SB 'liaison officer' whose job it is to acquaint himself with the problems of the groups concerned, the political aims and ideals of their clubs and organizations, to attend their meetings and demonstrations, and read their publications as well as understanding the political scene in the country of origin. Allied to this kind of work is the interviewing and approval of over one and a half thousand applications for British citizenship annually.

The main functions of the SB may be broadly defined as: dealing with treason, treachery, sedition, breaches of the Official Secrets Act, illegal drilling, rioting and the surveillance of all who may constitute a threat to the State. The latter usually fall into three main categories in addition to the foreign national groups already mentioned: people engaged in secret governmental or defence work, the leaders of subversive political organizations and the mentally disturbed who make threats against prominent public figures. SB men also act as bodyguards to national and international politicians and visiting heads of State; in this capacity they may well be proud of the fact that they have never lost a single celebrity under their protection. They also have to meet the request of any foreign embassy for special protection, or may even carry-out such duties on their own initiative if there is any danger of a real threat. Wherever possible, however, uniformed police are used for embassy duties, as the mere sight of the uniform acts as a deterrent, and also because the SB has been stretched to its limits over the past two years because of increasing waves of political violence, ranging from the attempted assassination of foreign diplomats to Arab and IRA letter-bombs and sundry explosions in the London area attributed to Irish political extremists and other activists devoted for whatever reason to the overthrow or embarrassment of the established government.

James Skardon, best-known of all MI5 interrogators. He was noted for his gentle methods of interrogation which broke many communist agents, including Klaus Fuchs the atom-spy.

UNITED STATES

The influence of the Intelligence agencies of the USA on internal and external politics has never been greater than it is today, for several good reasons: the agencies involved are among the biggest and most influential in the world (with the possible exception of the Russian KGB); they control to a large extent all the Intelligence Services of the NATO countries; and they pride themselves on being the most fanatical enemies of communism.

A general survey of US Intelligence reveals that it employs approximately 50,000 high-ranking personnel who in turn support several thousand agents of different nationalities around the world. The largest and most influential Intelligence organization is the *Central Intelligence Agency* (CIA) based at Langley, Virginia. Since its inception in 1947 it has grown in numbers and power at a great rate, so much so that Senators and Congressmen have demanded stricter governmental control over it on more than 150 occasions. In recent years it has even been labelled the 'Invisible Government', mainly because of the degree in which it has merged with the State Department and other government offices.

This formidable secret agency is directed by William Colby, a veteran Intelligence officer. Under diplomatic cover he has served as the CIA station head in Stockholm and Rome, and in Vietnam he conducted the 'pacification' programme and *Operation Phoenix*, which was aimed at the disruption and eventual destruction of the Vietcong infrastructure. According to Colby's own report (1971) over 20,000 Vietcong were killed while he was in charge of the operation.

Throughout his CIA career he has always remained very much in the background, his first public appearance being at the beginning of September 1973 when he was sworn-in at the White House as CIA Director. He began his Intelligence career with the war-time Office of Strategic Services (OSS), the fore-runner of the CIA, when he parachuted into Nazi-occupied Norway. Later, with the CIA, he became head of the

Allen Dulles, first director of the CIA.

Directorate of Operations, the department dealing with covert espionage and political operations.

Two of Colby's predecessors, Allen Dulles, who was the first director of the CIA, and Richard Helms, were also heads of the Directorate of Operations during their careers. Colby's activities in the Directorate earned him a reputation for being highly in favour of the more active, subversive operations usually associated with Intelligence work. Such operations were severely restricted by James Schlessinger, Colby's predecessor, but it is now thought that the new director may well start them again.

In addition to Vietnam the CIA has also been very active in

Richard Helms, ex-director of the CIA.

other Asian countries, notably Laos. In 1972, Long Cheng, a US base in that country was on the verge of being over-run by communist forces. The base was a 'prohibited area', especially for newsmen who wanted to report on the situation. It was later discovered that the strict secrecy at Long Cheng cloaked a CIA HQ which controlled a secret 'army' of 30,000 men. A similar base exists at Pakse in southern Laos.

Since 1962 Laos has been the centre of the CIA's biggest operation in any foreign country, an operation necessarily conducted under the strictest secrecy because of the Geneva Agreement, signed in 1962, which banned the use of foreign troops on Laotian territory. In spite of this the US government advocated active intervention to curb communist infiltration and influence in south-east Asia. The only way to achieve this was by the CIA's Directorate of Operations which promptly recruited, trained and financed an irregular fighting force organized into 'special guerilla unit' battalions of between 330 and 360 men.

It has also been alleged that in 1971 CIA-trained Laotian agents infiltrated up to 200 miles into the Chinese Peoples' Republic. Equipped with radios and wire-tapping apparatus the teams were sent out from a CIA base at Nam Lieu, a small, mountain valley airstrip in northern Laos. From there they were flown in stages, via other remote airstrips, to the Mekong river where they continued their journey by rubber dinghy.

The operations usually lasted three or four months, during which time radio contact was maintained with the Nam Lieu base and US Reconnaissance aircraft which flew along the Chinese border. Peking claims to have captured several teams and sent them back into Laos to work as double-agents.

In Europe the CIA spent several hundred million dollars on two radio stations which transmit to the Soviet Union and the communist satellite states. The stations, Radio Liberty and Radio Free Europe, were started in the early 1950s as a weapon in the 'Cold War'. Their original task was the transmission of anti-communist propaganda but they later developed into Intelligence-gathering centres for the CIA. Only a small percentage of the information supplied by a network of agents and informers is ever broadcast. Most of it is classified and ends up in the files of the CIA. Since the former

STRUCTURE AND ORGANIZATION OF THE SECRET SERVICES OF THE UNITED STATES

President of the USA

GOVERNMENT OF THE USA

NATIONAL SECURIT

COUNCIL FOR SECRET SERVICE ABROAD

CONTROL GROUP 54—12

JOINT SECRET SERVICES COMMITTEE

CIVILIAN DEPTS. OF THE SECRET SERVICE

STATE DEPT.

FEDERAL BUREAU OF INVESTIGATION (FBI)

SECRET SERVICE BRANCH OF ATOMIC ENERGY AUTHORITY

SECRET SERVICE BRANCHES OF

RECONNAISSANCE DEPT.

ADMIN. DEPT. FOR ESPIONAGE ANALYSIS

MINISTRY OF TRADE

MINISTRY OF AGRICULTURE

MINISTRY OF FINANCE

CUSTOMS AND EXCISE

TREASURY DEPT.

COASTGUARD DEPT.

CIA
CENTRAL INTELLIGENCE AGENC

DIRECTOR

DIRECTOR'S REPRESENTATIVE

SECTION I PERSONNEL AND ORGANIZATION

SECTION II ESPIONAGE AND INFORMATION

SECTION III SCIENCE AND TECHNICAL AFFAIRS

SECTION IV OPERATIONS DEPARTMENT

DEPT. FOR SECRET OPERATIONS

DEPT. FOR ANALYSIS OF INFORMATION

SUPERVISOR' COMMITTEE

CENTRE FOR SPACE OBSERVATIO

AVIATION AND SPACE RESEARCH AUTHORITY

SECTION 10/10 Reconnaissance overflights

NATO COUNTRIES

SEATO COUNTRIES

CENTO COUNTRIES

JAPAN

S. KOREA

S. VIETNAM

TAIWAN

SECRET SERVICE PRESIDENTIAL BODY GUARD

MILITARY BRANCH OF THE SECRET SERVICE

PENTAGON

MILITARY INFORMATION BUREAU

JOINT SECRET SERVICES COMMITTEE

DEPT. FOR SPECIAL OPERATIONS

ARMY   NAVY   AIR FORCE

G2 MIS CIC ONI DIO AIS OSI

NATIONAL SECURITY AGENCY (NSA)

1) Decoding Department for Government and Diplomatic Codes and Ciphers of the Armed Forces of the Soviet Union.

   Codes and Ciphers of Allies of the United States.

   Codes and Ciphers of neutral countries.

2) Department for Research and Development.

3) Secret Defence for Codes and Ciphers of the United States.

4) Personnel Department.

German Chancellor, Willy Brandt, had been endeavouring to form a closer relationship between his country and Poland, the Polish government has repeatedly requested the closure of the RFE base in Munich. The request is being given serious consideration by the West Germans.

On the strictly military intelligence side, the US Army Intelligence Services employ over 5,000 high-ranking agents, of which, according to *Army* magazine, published in Washington, (May 1967) 1,100 were at that time active in Vietnam. The Pentagon also has posted overseas 71 Military Attachés at US Embassies around the world.

Plan of the CIA tunnel under East Berlin, used to tap the telephone lines of the Russian HQ in the East sector. It was betrayed by George Blake (inset) a British Intelligence agent based in Berlin.

Key
A. Rudow cemetery
B. US radar station at Rudow
1. Schönefelderstrasse
2. Soviet telephone cables
3. Steel door
4. Phone-tapping equipment and amplifiers
5. Air conditioning plant
6. Steel door
7. Sandbags
8. Barbed-wire entanglement
9. Sandbags
10. East/West border

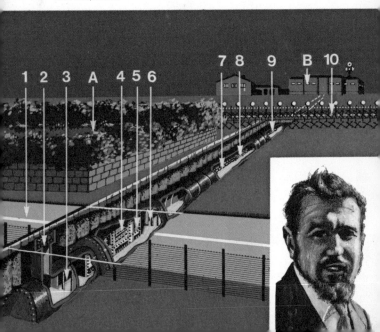

(*Left*) part of the interior of the tunnel under East Berlin. Built by the CIA, some of the equipment was supplied by British Intelligence. View shows amplifier banks, No. 4 on plan opposite. (*Right*) view of the tunnel at No. 8 on plan opposite.

The CIA's greatest internal rival, the *Defence Intelligence Agency* (DIA) founded in 1961 by Robert S. McNamara, inserted into the Intelligence field overseas its own experts who had already received years of experience in military reconnaissance. Since 1968, when Clark M. Clifford (who for many years was the Intelligence Adviser to the White House) became Secretary of Defence, this policy has been intensified.

As well as the CIA and DIA there are several other Intelligence agencies in the US, notably the G-2 Service which provides Intelligence for the US Army and Marine Corps; and the A-2 Service of the United States Air Force. The *National Security Agency* (NSA) at Fort Meade, in Maryland, acts as the code and cipher and radio control centre for all the Strike forces of the USA. Outside the US it maintains in all the countries bordering the communist bloc over 2,000 radio-monitoring stations, in addition to all the 'spy satellites' sent up by the United States.

At its Fort Meade HQ the NSA employs about 14,000 people,

1,000 of these being posted at various times to man its overseas listening posts. The Americans claim that this formidable espionage establishment and its outposts can monitor all communist military communications and are able to track the movements of nearly all units of the Warsaw Pact Armed Forces.

One of the major *coups* of the CIA took place in 1955 when together with the West German BND they 'tapped' the main Soviet telecommunications cables in the East Sector of Berlin.

In order to do this a tunnel 600 yards long was dug under the East/West border, beginning under a new radar station being built at Rudow in the West. This was chosen as the starting point for the venture as the removal of large quantities of soil from such a building-site would not attract the attention of the communist border guards only a few yards away.

It took almost three months to contruct it, a solid structure running 24 feet below street level, consisting of iron pipes seven feet in diameter which linked three large chambers, each sealed by electrically-operated security doors. These chambers contained the monitoring equipment, the telephone exchange switchboard and an air-conditioning plant. In addition it also had a recreation room for the agents. The main electricity supply was provided by the radar station at Rudow. Security devices abounded to safeguard the equipment, but in the worst type of emergency, the staff were given instructions to shoot their way out to the Western end of the tunnel.

The underground chambers were crammed with microphones, amplifiers, tape-recorders, teleprinters, and transformers. Some of the highly-sophisticated equipment was British made.

For over nine months US Army Corps and BND technicians and linguists working under CIA directions, tapped and recorded Intelligence communications in Russian, Polish, Czech and German. Amplifiers were used to boost the tapped messages in order to prevent any suspicion through loss of power in the signals. Over 400 conversations could be tapped at the same time.

During the following winter the tunnel was almost dis-

Soldier of the US 'Green Berets' and members of the CIA-run 'secret army' operating in Laos and Cambodia.

covered by the communists when the heat rising through the ground melted the snow along its entire length! A refrigeration unit was hastily installed along the ceiling.

On 22 April 1956, East German People's Police began to dig at the Eastern end, then Soviet Intelligence men took over and burst into the underground chambers. They were empty thanks to the highly efficient alarm system.

It was later disclosed that the discovery was no great surprise to the CIA; they had been expecting it for some time. A noticeable decline in telecommunications along the tapped lines had been previously noted, suggesting that the communists realized what was going on.

After its discovery the Soviets threw the tunnel open to public inspection and invited the Western Press to view it. For six weeks the admiring Russians conducted an estimated total of 40,000 people around the tunnel. Some were brought from as far away as Poland and the Soviet Union.

Counter-Espionage and National Security

The name of J. Edgar Hoover will always be synonymous with that of the world's most powerful and controversial agency for combating crime and espionage, the Federal Bureau of Investigation (FBI). For nearly fifty years he organized and directed almost single-handed this most formidable of law enforcement agencies. Serving under no fewer than eight Presidents, Hoover is remembered for his ruthless battles against the gangster underworld of the 1920s, his actions against the spies and traitors of the Second World War, and the vigilant upholding of American freedom against communist infiltration and subversion.

Hoover died in May 1972, leaving behind him a formidable crime-busting and security machine of his own making which, because of his own unstinting efforts has become noted for its efficiency.

For some time before his death, the FBI had been increasingly involved in the surveillance of civilians which seems to have gone beyond that required in the interests of national security. A fantastic array of electronic surveillance devices had been added to the FBI armoury and their very existence resulted in the use of illegal 'short-cuts' during investigations. Certain Government departments claimed they had a right to eavesdrop on anyone who might present the slightest threat to national security without seeking official permission first.

One case of unjustified surveillance came to light just before Hoover's death. A Congressional hearing was informed that the head of the FBI had for some time past been submitting secret memos to the President regarding the sex lives, drinking habits and intimate personal affairs of public figures. Hoover seems to have had an avid interest in such information and recorded every detail in the FBI files. Edited versions consisting of the most 'interesting' exerpts were forwarded to the President.

During the latter years of his service, Hoover proved to be something of a law unto himself, beyond even the control of the Administration and on occasions acting in defiance of it. Even President Nixon admitted that Hoover usually won the

J. Edgar Hoover, first director of the FBI.

Section of the FBI central files in Washington.

battle of wills over matters of national security and how the FBI should act in such affairs.

In 1970 a committee was formed at the order of President Nixon which consisted of the heads of all the US Intelligence departments with Hoover in charge as chairman. The aim of this inter-department body was the formulation of ideas for future Intelligence and Security operations to be conducted to counteract the recent civil disorders which had swept the United States. It was finally decided that a special intensive operation should be mounted which would include breaking into and entering certain premises and an increase in electronic surveillance. The proposal was given Presidential approval, but Hoover refused to have anything to do with it, and the idea was allegedly officially dropped although it still exists on paper and remains a highly-sensitive classified document.

Hoover's motives for defying the Presidentially-approved plan have never been established, but he further enforced his views by ordering the cessation of all FBI liaison with every US Intelligence agency involved at the meeting. This rash act seriously impaired the co-ordination so necessary for national security.

But this was by no means the end of Nixon's plans for an internal Intelligence operation. Three years later in 1973 an American newspaper published top secret White House

L. Patrick Gray, who became acting-director of the FBI after Hoover's death. He resigned soon afterwards.

STRUCTURE OF THE FEDERAL BUREAU OF INVESTIGATION (FBI)

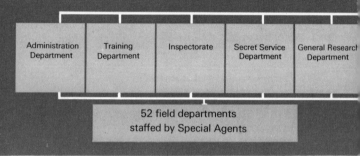

Administration Department	Training Department	Inspectorate	Secret Service Department	General Research Department

52 field departments
staffed by Special Agents

The above diagram is based on East German information.

documents which the President's spokesman conceded were authentic, and said that it was unfortunate that their confidentiality could not be maintained. The documents listed a range of clandestine actions against both American citizens and foreigners in the United States, all conducted 'in the interests of national security'; such actions as the breaking into of foreign embassies in Washington to procure vitally needed foreign cryptographic material and the interception of cables, telegrams and private telephone calls. One of the first victims of this policy seems to have been the Chilean embassy, closely followed by the office of Dr Daniel Ellsberg's psychiatrist, which was broken into in the search for anything related to the Pentagon Papers trial. It is also known that certain unfavourable reports on a number of prominent members of the Opposition found their way into the secret files of the White House.

Meanwhile, Hoover had been beset by his own internal problems. His new assistant, William Sullivan, disagreed with the FBI's pre-occupation with communism and what Hoover

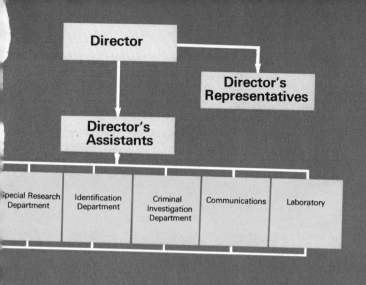

```
                    ┌──────────┐
                    │ Director │
                    └────┬─────┘
                         │        ┌─────────────────┐
                         │        │   Director's    │
                         │        │ Representatives │
                         │        └─────────────────┘
                    ┌────┴──────┐
                    │ Director's│
                    │ Assistants│
                    └─────┬─────┘
```

| Special Research Department | Identification Department | Criminal Investigation Department | Communications | Laboratory |

called 'the Red menace', to the detriment of Intelligence about matters of more immediate concern, such as the ever-increasing civil strife sweeping the United States. Hoover disagreed about the priorities and a feud developed which ended with Sullivan being forced into early retirement. He took with him, however, a complete set of documents which he presented to the Attorney-General and which eventually ended up in the White House. Sullivan implied that Hoover knew he himself was due to be retired but intended resisting any such attempt at removing him from office by using the documents as blackmail against the President. Oddly enough, Hoover did not seem to be aware that such important files were missing, and Nixon, knowing that they were now well out of FBI reach, did nothing and continued to support Hoover until his death in May 1972.

The FBI was not the only agency involved in the surveillance of civilians. It was revealed that in 1971 the Defence Department had ordered the Pentagon to curb its civilian spying activities. Military agents had been used to maintain computerized data-banks on civilians without the permission of the Defence Secretary. The Johnson Administration was blamed for starting the operation which smacked of 1984, and efforts were begun to eliminate 'prohibited information' from existing files. The extent of this clandestine spying operation may be gauged from a remark made by the Assistant Secretary of Defence, in which he stated that the task of sorting all the files would be 'monumental'.

Following Hoover's death, the post of FBI director remained vacant for a while. An acting-director, L. Patrick Gray, a lawyer friend of President Nixon, was nominated. Gray, however, did not last long; he became one of the long list of casualties of the Watergate Affair.

A great deal has been written about Watergate over the past year, and vast amounts of material published about the aftermath, but it is worth recounting the essential facts here with particular reference to CIA and FBI involvement, however indirect it may have been.

On 2 June 1972, five months before the US Presidential election, five burglars were caught in Washington's Watergate office building, the headquarters of the Democratic Party's national committee; all were in possession of an array of electronic surveillance and eavesdropping equipment and cameras. The culprits included an ex-CIA agent, Bernard Barker, who had been liaison officer between the CIA and anti-Castro groups in Florida; and James McCord, chief security co-ordinator for the Committee for the Re-election of the President (CREEP). It was later suggested that McCord may have been a CIA double-agent. He was promptly sacked from CREEP by former Attorney-General, John Mitchell, who had originally hired him. A matter of days later Mitchell resigned after his wife threatened to reveal 'certain dirty things that go on in politics'.

By this time an FBI investigation was in progress and other names began to emerge, including that of another CIA agent, Howard Hunt, former deputy chief of the Western Hemisphere section of the CIA. Three months later a total of seven people were indicted on a variety of charges including conspiracy, illegal eavesdropping and burglary. The Democrats tried in vain to exploit the affair but Nixon was re-elected by a landslide majority.

Soon after the election, the Watergate Hearing began which

resulted in the resignation of several White House advisers, aides and officials and the implication of a seemingly never-ending list of names of Administration personnel.

Patrick Gray admitted to destroying anti-Kennedy files which had been compiled by Howard Hunt, and had no option but to resign from the post of acting-Director of the FBI. Another acting-Director, William Ruckelshaus, was nominated by the President and held the post until June 1973 when the chief of the Kansas City Police, Clarence Kelly, took over as Director.

US Secret Service presidential bodyguard, a select body of agents responsible for the security of the President and his entourage. Consists of about 1,500 people of whom 860 are trained security agents whose sole task is to protect public figures from assassination.

WEST GERMANY

Intelligence Service

Unlike most countries West Germany has an adverse opinion of its Intelligence Service. The majority of the population seems to consider such a career as one of the lowest forms of employment which must inevitably attract and use personnel of a very dubious character. The bitter memories of the Nazi Secret Service, the *Gestapo* and *SD* are still too vivid. Secret Service work for the average German smacks too much of terror and atrocities committed secretly in the name of their country. Even politicians tend to shun espionage and security matters whenever possible.

No-one wants to know what goes on behind the high, grey walls of a former SS housing estate at Pullach, near Munich. Here, hidden from the outside world and guarded by watch-towers and dog patrols, is a compound containing a large complex of modern buildings, none of them more than two or three storeys high so that only their roofs can be seen from the road. Underground there exists a series of reinforced bunkers some of them extending three floors below the surface. This is the headquarters of the Federal Intelligence Agency – the *Bundesnachrichtendienst* (BND), directed by Gerhard Wessel and his deputy Dieter Blötz. The staff lives within the compound and their children attend a special school also within the confines of the headquarters. Security is maintained by electronically controlled doors and gates and electronic surveillance devices.

From this well-guarded compound Wessel commands a full-time staff of about 3,000 people, with another 2,500 distributed throughout the Federal Republic in various BND departments, and abroad under diplomatic cover. The most secret section of all, which directs the covert agents operating in the field abroad, notably in Eastern Europe, employs only a few hundred people. A further estimated 10,000 people work for the BND as informers; the whole organization covering West Germany in a vast network which is reputed to cost something in the region of 200 million marks to finance. Other BND departments are located in most large cities and towns where they operate under the cover of legally registered

WEST GERMAN INTELLIGENCE SERVICE

Federal Chancellery — Press Office

Bundesnachrichtendienst
FEDERAL INTELLIGENCE SERVICE *(BND)*
DIRECTOR of INTELLIGENCE

SECTION I	SECTION II	SECTION III	SECTION IV
Collection of Information	Technical Department	Evaluation Department	Central Office
Military	Radio Monitoring	Military	Administration
Political	Electronics	Political	
Economics	Monitoring of Foreign Transmitters	Economics	Organization
Armaments	Secret Technical Operations	Technical	Finance
Technical		Overt Collection of Information	
Counter-espionage	Radio Equipment	Dossiers	Legal
SUB-SECTIONS		SUB-SECTIONS	Economics
Soviet Union		Soviet Union	
East Germany	Photographic Laboratory	East Germany	Personnel
Poland		Poland	Training
Czechoslovakia	Printing Department	Czechoslovakia	
Other Warsaw Pact Countries		Other Warsaw Pact Countries	Public Relations
Middle East	Teleprinters	Middle East	Press Dept.
Far East		Far East	
Africa	Bugging Equipment	Africa	Security Guards
Latin America		Latin America	Couriers
Western Europe	Counter-bugging Equipment	Western Europe	
Northern Europe		Northern Europe	Computer Documentation
Southern Europe	Chemical Laboratory	Southern Europe	
North America		North America	Central Archives

companies and business enterprises, providing a 'front' for Wessel's agents.

Since 1968 when Wessel took command of West German Intelligence, it has had a very chequered history. Among its successes it can count the advance warning it provided of the invasion of Czechoslovakia by the armies of the Warsaw Pact countries. As early as May of that year BND agents had given firm indications that such intervention was more than likely. The CIA as good as ignored the information. One month later Wessel's agents reported that an invasion was imminent; the Americans labelled the information 'a fabrication'. It was not until 15 August that certain other Western Intelligence agencies began to realize that the BND was right. On 18 August twenty Warsaw Pact military divisions disappeared from view. The BND waited and then on the evening of 20 August Intelligence monitoring departments reported total radio silence from East European sources. Two hours later the Russians were in Prague.

US army camp at Oberursal near Frankfurt where Gehlen first began his Intelligence activities for the Americans.

Not so successful was the information on the riots in the Baltic ports of Poland in December 1970. Prior to this the BND had been instructed to concentrate on Intelligence from Poland, which was essential because of Chancellor Brandt's intention of visiting Warsaw in early December to sign a treaty of reconciliation with the Poles. Intelligence reports certainly showed a steep decline in the economic situation in Poland and that a rift was developing within the Government. But even these signs gave the BND no reason to expect the violence and bloodshed which ensued just before Christmas.

Brandt, who flew to Warsaw on 6 December, was appalled at the lack of reliable Intelligence on the internal situation there and the intrigues being conducted within the Government, which resulted in the downfall of his co-signatory and a complete change of Government a short time after his visit.

More recently it has become increasingly obvious that a reorganization of West German Intelligence is necessary with more clearly defined areas of operation and responsibility allocated.

The founder of this spy apparatus was General Reinhardt Gehlen, an ex-Nazi Intelligence officer who specialized during

Deutschland grüßt Euch!

unser Kameraden

German prisoners-of-war released from Soviet slave-labour camps. Until the mid-1950s they were a valuable source of information to Gehlen (inset) after they had been debriefed by Intelligence officers.

the war years in espionage against the Soviet Union. Immediately after the war, realizing the value of his accumulated knowledge and experience, he offered all the secret files of his former organization to the Americans. By 1946 he had been installed in a former Luftwaffe camp at Oberursal, near Frankfurt, at the head of an American-run Intelligence unit.

His first problem was finding enough people with Intelligence and Security training who had not been Nazis, the Americans having warned him not to use any *Gestapo* or *SD* personnel, but after scouring the prisoner of war camps he realized that such an order was unrealistic. He had to use men from these hated organizations simply because there were few others available with the necessary training in this type of work. Assumed identities were provided for any ex-*Gestapo* or *SD* officer Gehlen considered useful to his organization, a fact he managed to hide from his American masters. When it eventually became known publicly during the 1960s it only added to the scandals which forced him to resign as head of West German Intelligence.

Once an Intelligence organization had been formed and trained Gehlen was eager to infiltrate his agents once more into the Soviet Union, but the Americans considered his ideas to be impossible. Instead he had to be content with dealing with East Germany only, but even so one of his agents managed to penetrate as far East as Wrocław (formerly Breslau) in Poland. There he was arrested by Polish Security and spent two years in prison from where he escaped and made his way home in 1950.

In spite of his ideas for espionage operations, Gehlen was severely restricted in his activities by the Americans and the forays behind the Iron Curtain were nowhere near as frequent as he would have liked. For a while he contented himself with collecting as much Intelligence as possible on Eastern Europe from people who had once lived there on former German territory. The areas of particular interest now formed part of the Peoples' Republics of Poland and Czechoslovakia.

Even more valuable from the Intelligence point of view

Schloss Kransberg where the Americans set up a rival Intelligence unit competing against Gehlen.

Main administration building at BND headquarters, Pullach.

was the information to be gleaned from repatriated prisoners of war who had spent several years in Russian captivity. By 1947 a few had begun to return home and during the next few years about three million had been released. Under the pretence of being either social or welfare workers Gehlen's interrogators collected a mass of first-hand information on the Soviet Union, much of it of strategic value dealing with ports, railways, mines and factories where the prisoners had been employed as slave labour.

Gradually Gehlen increased the efficiency and activities of his Intelligence network until by 1951 he was prepared to mount a short-term mission inside Russia. The first two agents were themselves Russian, one being a Red Army deserter and the other a former prisoner of war. They were parachuted into Moldavia with instructions to stay for three weeks before making their way to Turkey where the CIA had arranged for their transportation back to West Germany. A few brief radio messages were picked up by the Intelligence receiving stations, then silence. Some months later Moscow Radio announced the execution of the two agents who had been arrested before reaching their destination. This infiltration operation was intensified during 1952 and culminated in a joint BND/CIA/SIS venture in which agents were landed by boat on the Baltic coast. The scheme was abandoned during the late 1950s.

In spite of Gehlen's dedication and the many successes of his agents, the CIA was steadily losing interest in the German Intelligence Service. Understandably they were beginning to object to financing operations of benefit to Bonn first and Washington last. They also did not like the high rate of loss of agents in East Germany. The communist Ministry for State Security (MfS) and the agents of its Security Service, the SSD, were becoming a power to be reckoned with.

By 1956 Gehlen's organization received official recognition from Bonn and was given the title of Federal Intelligence Service, with Gehlen receiving the title of 'President'. He immediately set about overhauling the existing departments, merging several smaller ones and creating new ones.

For the next six years the BND operated quite successfully, penetrating in certain cases as far afield as Iran, Africa and

Interior of the radio station at Pullach which links the BND HQ with its agents at home and abroad.

Afghanistan. Then, during the 1960s, things began to go drastically wrong. There occurred a series of scandals which ended with Gehlen's resignation as President of the BND.

It began with what became known as the *Felfe Affair*, which involved three BND employees being exposed as communist agents. Heinz Felfe, being head of the BND counter-espionage section, had effectively rendered Gehlen's efforts in this field completely useless. Several agents in East Germany were arrested by the SSD, others had to cease operations or escape across the frontier as best they could. A complete network was liquidated and the efforts of the BND brought almost to a standstill.

It did not increase Gehlen's popularity at home or abroad when it became known that the three double agents were all ex-*SS* men and formed part of an *SS* 'old boys' clique within West German Intelligence. This was well-known to Gehlen from the very early days at Oberursal, but as far as possible he kept this information quiet for obvious reasons. A rigorous 'purge' of all ex-*SS* personnel was the inevitable result, which

(*Left*) Heinz Felfe, former head of BND counter-espionage and (*right*) Hans Clemens, formerly attached to the BND's district office in Karlsruhe. Both were double-agents working for the Russians and their arrest ultimately resulted in Gehlen's resignation.

(*Left*) Dieter Blötz, who became Vice-President of the BND in 1970 and (*right*) Gerhard Wessel, Gehlen's successor as head of the BND.

deprived the BND of some of its best and longest-serving officers.

Even before any of this became public knowledge the head of the BND was in trouble, this time over the *Spiegel Affair*, which had been deliberately engineered by Gehlen but had gone horribly wrong. Strauss, the Minister of Defence, and Gehlen had for some time been at loggerheads, both sides looking for an opportunity to officially denounce the other. Gehlen made the first move by providing *Der Spiegel* magazine with material which exposed Strauss's policy in connection with German demands for nuclear weapons. When published in the magazine the German government took it as a case of treason. The editorial offices were raided, the proprietor and several editors arrested and duly charged with treasonable offences, the whole operation being conducted by Strauss. Adenauer, the Federal Chancellor, was informed and after listening to Strauss's version of the affair ordered the arrest of his Chief of Intelligence – Gehlen. No legal evidence for such drastic action was forthcoming and the idea was finally dropped, but not before the spy chief had been humiliated by being detained overnight under police escort at the Chancellery in Bonn.

Main entrance to West German Intelligence headquarters.

Five ministers resigned as a result of the *Spiegel* affair. The arrested editors were released and charges against them dropped. But it did not stop there; Strauss himself was soon to resign to be followed by Adenauer a year later.

Gehlen never recovered from this far-reaching scandal. The new Chancellor, Erhardt, openly despised the Federal Intelligence Agency and immediately ordered drastic cuts in the BND expenditure and a thorough investigation of its organization and activities. No doubt he would also have liked to retire Gehlen, but no successor was readily available; he continued as BND president until May 1968 when he retired to be succeeded by Gerhard Wessel.

Security Service

For some years after the war, the Allied authorities in West Germany considered forming a special department which would eventually be used to protect the constitutional order of the Federal Republic. But it was not until 1950 that such a department finally came into being. Known officially as the Office for the Protection of the Constitution (*Bundesamt für Verfassungsschutz* or BfV), it came directly under the jurisdiction of the Minister of the Interior. Each of the ten States which formed the Federal Republic had its own BfV office, the central administration and co-ordination department being set up in a new building on Bruckenstrasse in the centre of Cologne.

The function of the BfV was defined as the collection of information relating to any attempted undermining of the constitutional order. One problem, however, remained. Who was to be the director of this newly-formed political police force? A large proportion of the nominated candidates were immediately rejected because of their Nazi past. Finally a certain Dr Otto John was nominated and accepted. Many prominent politicians bitterly resented this choice as John was noted for his violently anti-Nazi past and had worked for the British during the war broadcasting 'black propaganda' against his own country. He was regarded by many Germans as a traitor. His popularity did not increase when it became known that he had also interrogated several senior Nazis on behalf of the British in preparation for the forthcoming war-crimes trials. John had previously received training in International and German Law and was frequently consulted while the long series of trials lasted.

The appointment of Director of the BfV came as something of a shock to him, but he accepted nevertheless. Protests were made immediately to the Bonn government accusing John of a multitude of crimes ranging from being a secret agent of the British and the communists, to being an alcoholic and homosexual. The new president of West Germany, Theodor Heuss, supported John wholeheartedly and requested him to vet candidates for governmental posts. This only served to increase his unpopularity as the candidates were frequently rejected on the grounds of their past Nazi activities. John's job was not made any easier by the fact that the Federal Chancellor of the time, Dr Konrad Adenauer, was not at all happy with having John as director of the BfV.

The first problem to be surmounted by the new department was the selection of suitable agents and staff; this was no easy task as most of the security experts had been either members of the *Gestapo* or *SD*. It became unavoidable that some of these people had to be employed as no others were available who had Security or Intelligence backgrounds.

In its original form the BfV consisted of three departments: the first dealt with administration and legal affairs; the second concentrated on the collection of information, employing plain-clothed agents whose duty it was to attend all political rallies and meetings, join and observe at close quarters extremist organizations, trade unions and communist refugee organizations; the third department was the evaluation section which examined all the information submitted by Department II, and drew up reports for the Minister of the Interior, the Public Prosecutor and the political section of the police. It also co-ordinated the work of the ten local State offices of the BfV.

For three years John and his agents worked unstintingly with some notable successes to their credit. Then, one day in 1953, he received a summons to attend a midnight meeting of high-ranking politicians and government officials. After some preliminary pleasantries the Prime Minister announced that at that moment the police were carrying out mass-arrests at the order of the Public Prosecutor. John was astounded to learn that a militant neo-Nazi group operating within the German Youth Organization (BDJ) had been exposed which engaged in infiltrating youths into East Germany and secret night-time military training under CIA direction.

The assembled officials accused the BfV director of shielding the group and aiding and abetting their activities. Several referred to him as a tool of the CIA. The BfV had been made to look ridiculous and John did the only thing possible: propose a joint American/German investigation into the affair. This was promply accepted.

Meanwhile, in East Germany, large numbers of youths were arrested, accused of espionage and subversion, and of being members of the BDJ/CIA militant organization. Many received sentences of ten years hard labour, while in the Federal Republic the BDJ was promptly disbanded and proscribed.

Four years after being appointed director of the BfV, John was involved in an intriguing affair which has never been satisfactorily cleared up. In 1954, while in West Berlin, he disappeared. One week later he broadcast on the East German Radio and announced that he had defected and a press conference was arranged at which he appeared and gave his reasons for changing sides. In 1955 he suddenly re-appeared in West Germany claiming that he had been kidnapped and that the press conference was conducted under duress. From East Berlin, he had been transported to the Soviet Union, where he underwent interrogations to determine whether 'Kim' Philby was in fact a triple agent betraying the Russians to British Intelligence. He maintained that the KGB never asked him about his work as BfV director.

His story was not believed and the double-defector received a four year prison sentence for 'treasonable offences'. Since his release he has been fighting unsuccessfully for a re-trial to clear his name.

In 1964 the BfV underwent a radical change. It was re-housed in a large office block on Innere Kanal Strasse, with a greatly increased staff of over 1,000 people distributed in

Otto John, former head of the BfV who 'defected' to East Berlin. He appeared at a press conference surrounded by East German State Security agents.

five departments under Dr Günther Nollau, who, during conversations with journalists, has stated that the BfV estimates the number of communist agents operating in West Germany at 15,000 at any given time. Of these less than 3,000 are identified and arrested. In 1965 a wide variety of agents were involved in espionage activities on behalf of several countries: 239 for the USSR, 44 for the Czechs, 32 for the Poles, as well as many other nationalities. In the case of 16 arrested agents it was never determined for whom they were spying.

The years 1968–69 were vintage years for the BfV. Hardly a week passed without some 'security scare' hitting the headlines. It was during this time that the Ministry of Defence suffered badly as one official after another 'committed suicide' or 'met with a fatal accident'. Many of the deaths were indeed linked with espionage and security matters of the highest order. The scare reached such proportions that Dr Kiesinger and Herr Willy Brandt decided to investigate thoroughly the Federal Intelligence Services.

A few days after this was announced, three communist agents pulled off one of the most audacious spy *coups* of the century. It was discovered that they had driven several hundred kilometres through West Germany with the nose of a stolen NATO missile 10 feet long sticking through the rear-window of their car. At the Iron Curtain it had been dismantled, packed into crates and sent by air-freight to Moscow.

It was eventually revealed to the public that there was possibly a reason for these months of seemingly never-ending

Willy Brandt accompanied by Security agents.

During visits of foreign politicians and Heads of State to West Germany the *'Popo'* agents are much in evidence. With binoculars they survey the crowds and keep special watch on known political 'agitators'.

espionage and suicide scandals. This concerned an officer of Czech Intelligence who had defected when his country was invaded by the Warsaw Pact Armies. His intended destination was Bonn, but he had spent some time *en-route* in Austria where he divulged the names of several German and Austrian officials who were working for the communists. It looked as if some of them at least realized that they had been betrayed and committed suicide rather than face the scandal of a trial. Others promptly defected to the East; six communist agents succeeded in returning home undetected, which led to the accusation that the BfV had allowed them to escape after having had them under surveillance for several weeks. The official reason given for this long series of security 'lapses' was that 'extreme rivalry' existed between the competing

Intelligence Services: BfV, BND, MAD (Military Counter-espionage) and the Political section of the police.

Political Police

The West German uniformed police also has its own Intelligence Service in the form of the Political Police, popularly referred to as the 'Popo'. Officially the agents of this section come under the jurisdiction of the criminal police but their activities are never publicized in the same way as are, for example, the exploits of the murder squad.

In each of the states of West Germany this political section exists under a different name; in Berlin it is known as *Abteilung I*, while in Munich it exists as *KA III*. The most important department operates in Bonn where it is known as *K 14* and employs approximately 300 agents under a certain Wilhelm Krome, who is described as a 'criminal adviser'. The main duties of *K 14* and its counterparts throughout the Federal Republic have been defined as 'the protection of politicians, both foreign and German, and the detection/prevention of all criminal acts against the Security Regulations'.

One of their more mundane tasks is the collection of politically subversive documents. Vast files are kept of such literature, *Abteilung I* in Berlin being apparently in possession of the biggest collection consisting of about 20,000 documents. These are kept on file for a period of 15 years.

Most of the efforts of the *Popos* are necessarily kept secret, although it is known that they frequently use electronic devices and miniature cameras during the course of their duties. They are always to be seen at state visits in Bonn, surveying the crowds through binoculars; during demonstrations they hide themselves at vantage points from which to take photographs of the demonstrators for their files. It has even been known for them to infiltrate meetings and demonstrations. One ruse used by *Abteilung I* was to disguise its agents as ordinary traffic police along the route in order to overhear conversations. A less successful subterfuge was employed by an agent of *KA III* in Munich. He donned a long-haired wig and jeans and joined a demonstration march. While attempting to provoke the marchers into attacking the police he became involved in an argument during which his wig became dislodged. He was rescued from the irate mob by his colleagues in the criminal department.

Unlike the uniformed police the *'Popos'* do not present any kind of reports for parliamentary examination, and this has led to many adverse comments being made about them by German politicians. They are noted for shunning any kind of publicity, even more so than their colleagues in the BfV. Because of this official secrecy which surrounds their activities they have acquired the unwanted image of a present-day *Gestapo*, an image hotly resented by their officers. They strongly deny the popular idea that they are 'snooping' into everyone's affairs, maintaining that they are 'special protectors of order' and that they should not be thought of as anything other than an ordinary police department such as the fraud or vice squads, which also have special tasks to perform.

It may be argued that the special tasks of the *'Popos'* necessitate the use of 'special methods', for they are concerned not with ordinary crime but with matters of state security. This must necessarily entail a great deal of secrecy. It is for this reason that Germans are reminded of the activities of the Nazi *Gestapo* and draw their own erroneous conclusions about their Political Police Force.

'Popo' agent photographing a demonstration.

FRANCE

Until 1958 the French Secret Service was divided into several sections which more often than not overlapped each other's territory and performed similar functions. The most widely known department is the *Deuxieme Bureau*, which, contrary to popular belief, is not the official name of the French Intelligence Service, although it is intimately concerned with Intelligence. It's main function, however, is the centralization and interpretation of Intelligence material specifically intended for the French Armed Forces. For this purpose it has two main departments which provide the information to be assessed for the High Command. These are the *Service de Reseignements*, which is the French Military Intelligence apparatus, and a counter-espionage service. Together, these two departments form the Special Services.

Very little is ever made public of the activities of the Special Services in peacetime; only during time of war do they assume a more prominent, public role, when their joint title changes to that of the Fifth Bureau of the French General Staff.

During the late 1950s and early 1960s the French Government drastically re-organized its Intelligence Services and Security Departments in order to suit them for extensive operations in Moslem countries with which France was deeply involved at the time politically. Two major agencies emerged from the re-shuffling of various departments: the *Service de Documentation Exterieure et de Contre-Espionage* (SDECE) and the *Direction de la Surveillance Territoire* (DST).

The DST fulfils the function of an internal security service and counter-espionage department, roughly approximating the duties of the British Security Service (DI5), while the former acts as the covert 'spy' agency for collecting Intelligence and operating agents outside France.

It is indeed unfortunate that the only time the SDECE is mentioned in the Press it seems to be involved in some major scandal or other. In late 1971 it made world headlines when accused of being deeply involved in narcotics and counterfeit currency dealings; and ever since its inception in 1958 it has had its public image badly tarnished, the first major outcry being against its involvement in the kidnapping and subsequent murder of an Algerian political leader in very unsavoury circumstances. The resulting journalistic reports on the affair in various countries and the public outrage against the SDECE very nearly brought about the downfall of the de Gaulle administration in France.

The Intelligence agencies of other Western countries in recent years have had a very poor opinion of the French Secret Service owing to the wide-spread belief that it has been, and still is, heavily penetrated by the KGB.

According to one British source, the SDECE is divided into five sections. Section 1 deals with Intelligence and it is in turn sub-divided into seven departments, each prefixed with the letter 'R' (for *Reseignement*). The most interesting and unorthodox department is without doubt 'Service Five', popularly known as the 'Action Service'. During the OAS terror in Algeria and France the strong-arm squad of this department performed the necessary unpleasant tasks which included kidnapping, assassination and interrogation (usually accompanied by torture) to combat the terrorists of the OAS. Its agents are taught everything there is to know about interrogation, sabotage, demolition and destruction in general. These men, known as the *'Barbouzes'*, have become hated and feared for their ruthlessness and brutality. They perform most of the tasks which in the Soviet Union are assigned to the KGB Department of Special Tasks, erroneously known as *'Smersh'*.

In 1968 the former head of the American Section of the SDECE, a certain M de Vosjoli, created a furore by defecting to the Americans and announcing that John F. Kennedy, while he was the President of the United States, had sent to President de Gaulle a letter in which he stated that he had reliable information to the effect that the SDECE and French Cabinet had been infiltrated by the KGB. De Gaulle, for reasons best known to himself, practically ignored the disclosures. He did, however, send an emmissary to the United States, a General de Rougement. In Washington de Rougement learned that the source of Kennedy's information was a KGB defector. Under interrogation the defector astounded de Rougement with his disclosures of details known to Soviet

Intelligence about the activities and staff of the SDECE.

Before long the French interrogator ascertained that Soviet agents in the NATO Headquarters near Paris were in a position to produce for Moscow any document required by the Soviet Secret Service. It soon became apparent that the KGB almost certainly had a complete set of all NATO secret documents.

Following this the defector further revealed that he and his former directors in Moscow were fully aware of the details of the 1958 re-organization of the SDECE, and that the French Ministry of the Interior and the Ministries of Foreign Affairs and Defence had all been infiltrated by Soviet agents. As the interrogations intensified, a vast Soviet espionage net came to light. A nationwide network of agents in the pay of the

Roger Barberot, head of a mysterious French Intelligence 'cover' organization.

Kremlin operating under the code-name *'Sapphire'*, a network which included French Intelligence Officers, NATO employees, and even a high-ranking politician in de Gaulle's Government, was revealed.

In spite of these seemingly damning disclosures about the vast Intelligence operation being conducted from KGB Headquarters in Moscow against the Government of France, almost nothing was done about it by either the SDECE or DST. The whole affair gradually sank into obscurity and was soon forgotten by all except the Allied Intelligence Services. There can be little doubt that the Secret Services of Western Europe and the United States breathed a sigh of relief when not long afterwards France withdrew from NATO completely.

The French reaction to British and American Press comments on the whole affair was to label them as a 'revenge campaign' directed against the de Gaulle Administration by the CIA. Their explanation was that it came in retaliation to a purge of French agents working for the CIA and FBI within French Intelligence, a purge ordered by de Gaulle himself. The whole *'Sapphire Affair'* was dismissed by the French as 'completely ridiculous and of the highest absurdity'.

In 1971 a senior French Intelligence agent was arrested in the United States at Newark, New Jersey, and charged with conspiring with one other to smuggle heroin valued at £5 million. The men were later revealed to be Colonel Paul Fournier, allegedly No. 2 in SDECE, and Roger Delouette, a former SDECE agent. They both claimed to be acting on behalf of one of the directors of French Intelligence.

Not long afterwards other SDECE activities of a disreputable nature were disclosed to the world. It was widely claimed that French Intelligence was engaged in large-scale drug trafficking to augment its funds. In Haiti an SDECE agent was arrested when 106 kilos of heroin were found in his car; Michel Mertz, another agent, was imprisoned for 5 years on narcotics charges. Rumours abounded to the effect that French Intelligence was deeply involved in passing counterfeit currency, $17,400 having been found at the home of an agent's girl-friend. It is not really surprising that the SDECE accuses the CIA and FBI of carrying out a vendetta against French agents on American territory.

The identity of Paul Fournier was disclosed by Colonel Roger Barberot, a former French ambassador, who has, since 1968, held a rather intriguing post, that of Director of the mysterious 'Bureau for the Development of Agricultural Production'. This Bureau is, to all outward appearances, run by the French Ministry of Foreign Affairs, but it is generally believed to be a cover organization for an Intelligence department.

As a result of the numerous accusations levelled against the SDECE around the world at this time, its Director, Alexandre de Marenches, was interrogated in Paris by an examining magistrate, to be closely followed by several other past and present Secret Service Executives.

Meanwhile, a former Minister of Defence, General Pierre Billotte, was demanding that the SDECE be disbanded and completely re-organized from scratch. He claimed publicly that too many 'shady and corrupt characters' were involved in the running of the Intelligence apparatus and that too many 'foreign influences' were being exerted on its agents, this being an obvious reference to the CIA/FBI agents in the employ of the Secret Service mentioned earlier.

On the credit side, the French Intelligence Service has had some notable successes behind the Iron Curtain, particularly in Rumania. In 1965 they recruited a female agent who was employed by the government Statistical Office, a post which enabled her to travel freely and visit numerous government establishments. During these frequent travels she made a point of befriending as many officials as time would permit; she encouraged her male companions to talk freely of State matters. Concealed on her person was another constant 'companion:' a hair-wire recording device. For five years this agent provided the SDECE with invaluable inside information with the aid of this instrument.

Unfortunately for the SDECE she had acquired a taste for the West on her visits with official delegations, and finally defected in 1970, much to the chagrin of her masters in Paris.

Before France resigned from the NATO Pact, it came to light that a Soviet agent was at work in the NATO Headquarters near Paris. This information was provided by Michał Goleniewski, a defector from Polish Intelligence who named

Roger Delouette, French Intelligence agent arrested in the US on drug-smuggling charges.

the agent as Georges Pacques, at that time Deputy Director of the NATO Press Service.

The DST examined Goleniewski's evidence and decided to introduce a female security agent to Pacques to discover as much as possible about his activities. The DST agent was very soon on intimate terms with the traitor and waited until she knew he was in possession of classified documents. Then the waiting security officers pounced.

Recently the French Secret Service seems to have become something of a 'State within a State' operating almost entirely outside the laws of the French Republic and beyond Governmental control.

ISRAEL

The origins of *Shai*, the Israel Intelligence Service which served the underground Jewish army in Palestine after the war, are not known. For years the British Mandate authorities attempted to discover the whereabouts of its headquarters and the identities of its leaders, without success. This phantom army of agents intercepted all military, police and British Intelligence coded messages and transmissions. They already had almost complete sets of secret British Intelligence files relating to Palestine.

For some time the files of *Shai*, which the British had tried so desperately to locate, were hidden in an apartment on Jabotinski Street in Tel Aviv. Later, they were sealed into a specially-built chamber in the basement of a newly-constructed hospital, where they remained until 1947 when the UN General Assembly authorised the creation of the State of Israel.

A year later a meeting was convened at 85 Gordon Street in Tel Aviv. Outwardly the building was just an ordinary block of flats on a street corner, occupied by ordinary Israeli families. On the third floor, however, there was a door bearing the inscription *Veterans' Counselling Service*. This was the headquarters of *Shai*.

At the meeting arrangements were made for the complete reorganization of the Intelligence Service. *Shai* was officially disbanded and a new apparatus formed which consisted of three main departments. The first was subdivided into two sections, *Aman*, for Military Intelligence and *Raman*, counter-espionage. Department II was to be the Political Section of the Foreign Ministry; and Department III, *Shin Beth*, the Internal Security Service.

Bloodshed and strife marked the early years of the existence of Israel: it was a hectic time for the newly-created Secret Service. Its directors had no access to training and operational details on which to base their organization, and no other nation was willing to impart such information. The Israelis had to evolve their own techniques, a situation which, coupled with the internal strife, tended to make the agents over-zealous and it was some time before they learned the value of being

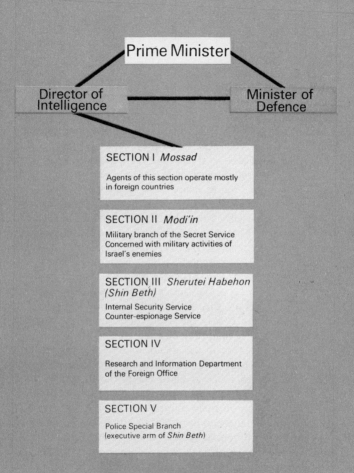

ISRAELI INTELLIGENCE SERVICES

Prime Minister

Director of Intelligence — **Minister of Defence**

SECTION I *Mossad*

Agents of this section operate mostly in foreign countries

SECTION II *Modi'in*

Military branch of the Secret Service
Concerned with military activities of Israel's enemies

SECTION III *Sherutei Habehon (Shin Beth)*

Internal Security Service
Counter-espionage Service

SECTION IV

Research and Information Department of the Foreign Office

SECTION V

Police Special Branch
(executive arm of *Shin Beth*)

discreet. From these seemingly disorganized beginnings there evolved a Secret Service which is today the envy of most Intelligence Services around the world, a Service which is one of the most secret in existence, with a reputation for being highly efficient – and deadly. The very existence of *Shin Beth* was kept a closely-guarded secret for nine years, until the Israeli Prime Minister announced it in parliament in 1957.

Six years earlier a change had taken place within the Intelligence Service. The Political Department was found to be inadequate and had to be disbanded, and another department was needed with much wider 'interests'. To this end *'Mossad'* was formed with instructions to act as a general Intelligence agency and to avoid the mistake its predecessor had made of concentrating too much on foreign political Intelligence. *Mossad* and *Shin Beth* soon formed a close working-relationship, a situation which does not exist in many countries where the Intelligence and Security Service consider themselves as rivals. They expanded rapidly and today direct a vast network of agents around the world with several bases set up in many West European cities. Most Israeli agents operate under false names and hold false passports, supposedly issued by the governments of friendly countries. In 1973 their government received a sharp protest from the British when it was discovered that *Mossad* agents were using British passports while engaged in 'anti-Arab activities' in Bierut. The KGB has disclosed that it believes Israeli Intelligence to be active in no less than seventy countries, while the CIA has complimented it by referring to it as 'one of the best in the world' and admitting that they know less about it than they do about the KGB.

For five years *Mossad* had one of its best agents operating inside Egypt. Posing as a wealthy horse-breeder, Wolfgang Lötz, took up residence in Cairo where the Egyptians were convinced that he was a former Nazi *SS* officer accused of war crimes hiding in their country. He did not correct their erroneous belief. Instead, he used it to gather around himself a select circle of influential friends which included government, military and police officials who informed him, in strictest confidence, of course, of the military projects underway in Egypt under the guidence of German experts, and the political aims of their country. His friends never dreamed that every word was being transmitted back to Israel by Lötz.

Execution of Elie Cohen in Martyrs' Square, Damascus.

Eventually the flow of top secret information reached saturation point and he had to leave the country for a while in order to pass on the accumulated Intelligence, but the evening before his intended departure, Lötz was arrested by Egyptian Security agents. A search of his villa revealed all the paraphanalia of espionage and it was later established that his transmissions had been intercepted and located by the agents of another power who dutifully informed Egyptian Security.

Elie Cohen, another expert Israeli agent, operated alone in Syria before being arrested, and was ultimately responsible for much of the Intelligence which enabled the Israelis to defeat Syria in a matter of hours during the Six Day War in 1967. For three years he provided information from official scources, until one day a radio detector van picked-up his transmissions.

The trial which followed aroused world public opinion, but the Syrian court was determined to be merciless. They turned Cohen's execution into a public spectacle. A gallows was erected in Martyrs' Square, Damascus, where in a blaze of floodlights, in front of a crowd of several thousands, he was hanged at midnight on 18 May 1965.

(*Left*) Wolfgang Lötz and (*right*) Elie Cohen.

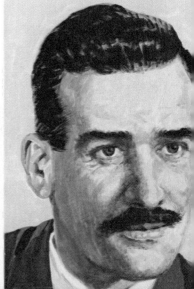

EGYPT

During the early 1950s agents of the CIA searched the Arab world for a suitable leader of the Arab nations, someone who, with CIA aid, could overthrow King Farouk of Egypt and emerge as the dominant leader of the Arabs backed by the United States. They eventually discovered Colonel Gamel Nasser who took a great interest in the American ideas for the future of his country and the Arab world in general; the desired revolution took place in 1952 with Colonel Neguib acting as Nasser's 'puppet'. In the wake of the internal upheaval came an influx of CIA agents, supposedly to act as 'advisers' to the new régime. It was not long before Nasser invited his 'advisers' to reorganize the Egyptian armed forces and Intelligence Services, the main department of which was to be closely modelled on the CIA and named the *General Intelligence Agency* (GIA). Electronic espionage and surveillance apparatus was shipped over from the United States and upon CIA advice several former Nazi Intelligence officers were employed as instructors in the use of the equipment. This was mainly because the CIA did not wish to be too openly involved and invite criticism from other countries, notably Israel.

Meanwhile, Nasser went behind the backs of the Americans and concluded an arms deal with the Soviet Union, thus giving the Russians a firm foot-hold on Arab territory and in their

Salah Nasr, former head of Egyptian Intelligence. Interrogated Lötz in Cairo after his arrest. Nasr was himself arrested after the Six-Day War in 1967 together with most of his henchmen and accused of being responsible for the Egyptian defeat. He was charged with falsifying Intelligence reports, using public funds for his personal use and the torture of innocent people arrested by his agents.

internal affairs. By the time the CIA discovered what was going on it was too late. Then, in 1956 came the final blow. Without any previous warning or consultation with Washington, a combined force of Israeli, British and French troops attacked Egypt and seized control of the Sinai Peninsula and advanced to the Suez Canal. The US Government was enraged at the audacity of the attack, especially as the CIA had been saying for some time that such military action was impossible. The Americans attempted a hasty withdrawal from the scene without losing too much influence in the Arab world, but because of the CIA bungling the damage had already been done. The trust which the CIA had put in Nasser had been rather naïve and the Russians had now succeeded in taking over in the role of 'advisers'. The Allied invasion turned out to be a fiasco anyway, and Nasser continued to rule the Arabs under Soviet instructions.

The Intelligence Agencies which the CIA established for the Egyptians consist of two main departments, each of which is further divided into several sections and subsections; the main department, already mentioned, being the GIA, or *Muhabbarat-El-Amma* to give it its Egyptian title.

Over the years this organization has become notorious and feared for its regular use of terror-tactics, torture and murder during the course of its activities both at home and abroad. As well as conducting 'operations' in other countries it fulfils roles on Egyptian territory, mainly in the field of counter-espionage and on occasions in normal police functions.

At the beginning of the late President Nasser's régime, the spying activities of the Egyptian Secret Service reached absurd proportions, resulting in a vast espionage apparatus which was consequently badly organised, badly co-ordinated and hopelessly inefficient. Vast sums of money were squandered on the most bizarre operations ranging from attempted revolutions in various countries to the projected assassination of several foreign politicians and leaders. The large numbers of agents used in these operations ensured that nothing Egyptian Intelligence tried to do remained secret for very long.

The second Intelligence department, *Mabahes El-Amma,* is the Security Service, which has saturated Egypt with its

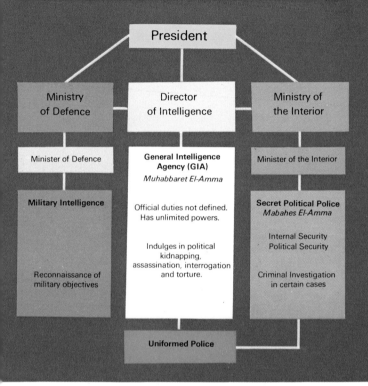

EGYPTIAN INTELLIGENCE SERVICES

President

Ministry of Defence — **Director of Intelligence** — **Ministry of the Interior**

Minister of Defence

General Intelligence Agency (GIA)
Muhabbaret El-Amma

Minister of the Interior

Military Intelligence

Official duties not defined. Has unlimited powers.

Secret Political Police
Mabahes El-Amma

Internal Security
Political Security

Indulges in political kidnapping, assassination, interrogation and torture.

Reconnaissance of military objectives

Criminal Investigation in certain cases

Uniformed Police

agents and informers; neither department respects the work of the other and they frequently refuse to work together or exchange information. It has even been known for them to deliberately sabotage each others activities.

Both departments rely heavily on an army of informers, paid and unpaid; in order to keep whichever section that employs them happy, it is quite common for them to fabricate information when nothing of interest occurs for them to report. In spite of the chaos which seems to prevail throughout the Service, it is nevertheless noted for being one of the most active and ruthless security organs in the world.

SOVIET UNION

Intelligence and Security Services

Probably the largest Intelligence Service in the world is that of the Soviet Union. It consists of two main departments, the best-known being the *KGB*, a vast organization embracing the tasks of internal security and foreign espionage which has been described as a multipurpose, secret power which extends far beyond its popular image in the west of a secret police force.

This is the main department of Soviet Intelligence, the other being its bitter rival the Intelligence section of the Red Army, known as the *GRU*.

KGB headquarters is located in a large building at 2 Dzerzhinsky Square in Moscow, known as the *Lubianka*. In Tsarist times it housed an insurance company, the KGB making good use of the former security vaults as interrogation and detention cells. *Lubianka* is in fact two adjoining buildings, the facade having been rebuilt to conceal where they connect. One houses the main administration offices of the KGB and the other the prison and interrogation section.

It is impossible to assess the number of people employed by Soviet Intelligence as it has so many ramifications and sections which have no counterpart in the west. One defector

'Lubianka', Russian Secret Police headquarters at 2 Dzerzhinsky Square in Moscow, consists of two adjoining buildings. One is the administrative offices of the KGB and the other the KGB prison for political prisoners. The exercise yard of the prison, divided by high walls into several small compounds, is located on the roof.

Some directors of the Soviet Secret Service: (*top left*) Beria; (*top right*) Semichastny; (*bottom left*) Shelepin; (*bottom right*) present head of the KGB, Yuri Andropov.

mentions a figure of 25,000 KGB personnel engaged in the espionage section alone. No doubt secret lists and estimates exist in the classified files of our Intelligence Services.

No other Secret Service in the world takes such great pains to select the right personnel for espionage and security training. The Russians believe that any intelligent person can, with the correct training, be turned into a first-class agent for work abroad. For this purpose they are prepared to devote ten years of intensive instruction in the customs and language of the country to be infiltrated. These highly specialized courses are held in spy schools at various places in the Soviet Union (see map for locations), the most famous being located at Gaczyna, where the agents are trained for work in the English-speaking countries. The school covers a large area of country sub-divided into sections containing replicas of typical western towns. The agents speak only English during the long years of their training, wear western clothes and live exactly as they will in the west when sent over as agents for the KGB. At the end of all this each agent can pass without difficulty as a native of the country in which he will operate.

'Gordon Lonsdale' was one of the best-known 'students' of this school who worked for many years in the west posing as an English businessman. In 1961 he was exposed as a Soviet agent and leader of the Portland spy ring. After spending some time in prison he was exchanged for an English business-man serving a labour camp sentence in the Soviet Union. Once home again he became the star of a film entitled *'The Dead Season'*, based closely on his espionage activities in the west. It gave an unprecedented view of the work at home and abroad of the Soviet Intelligence Services.

Lonsdale died of a heart attack in Moscow in 1970 and to this day the full extent of his activities in the west remains a mystery to our Security Services.

Another well-known KGB agent was Colonel Rudolf Abel who was actively engaged in espionage in the west for thirty years. He too had the misfortune to be arrested and like Lonsdale became a pawn in a 'Spy-swap' between east and west. Once back in Moscow the KGB made good use of his years of experience abroad and made him director of the English/American section of the KGB. It has also been reported that he personally supervized the training of future agents at Gaczyna.

Abroad, the KGB acts in a manner similar to that of its greatest rival, the CIA, influencing the internal and foreign policies of other nations and providing 'advisers' and material aid whenever necessary. Some of its most dangerous activities have been carried out right on the doorstep of the USA, in Cuba. In an operation very similar to the CIA 'interference' in Egypt, the Russians began in 1959 to infiltrate into Cuba and eventually succeeded in setting up an Intelligence Service

ORGANIZATION AND STRUCTURE OF THE SOVIET COMMITTEE FOR STATE SECURITY (KGB)

Central Committee

Council of Ministers

Chairman of the KGB

Central Secretariat

Legal Bureau

MAIN DIRECTORATES

1st. Internal Counter-Intelligence

2nd. Foreign Intelligence

3rd. Armed Forces Counter-Intelligence (formerly GUKR 'Smersh')

Border Troops (GUVPO)

Political (SPU)

Economic (EKU)

Transport

Surveillance

Communications

Special Investigations

Kremlin Commandant

Kremlin Guard

Atomic Energy Section (Section K)

SPECIAL SECTIONS

1st. Operational Files and Archives

2nd. Technical

3rd. Illegal Documents

4th. Telecommunications

5th. Telephone Taps

6th. Censorship

Administration and Supply

Personnel

Training

Communications

Government Communications

Kremlin Communications

Headquarters Commandant

Finance

Pensions

Clothing and Supply

Arms and Equipment

Medical

Transportation

Billeting

Construction

Agriculture

Entrance to KGB headquarters.

for Fidel Castro which could also be used for their own purposes. Known as the *Direccion General de Inteligencia* (DGI) it began operations in 1961 shortly before Castro announced his belief in Marxism. In spite of this he refused to be totally subservient to Moscow and insisted that the main section of the DGI should be an organization for promoting revolutionary activities abroad using guerrilla tactics, and not an Intelligence gathering agency as the Russians wanted. He got his way and the DNL was set up within the framework of the DGI.

The activities of these organizations began in earnest in 1962 with operations in Brazil, Venezuela, Peru and Colombia. Not one of them was successful. The nearest the Soviet-trained agents came to achieving a *coup* was in the Dominican Republic in 1965. In this case the DGI operatives had been trained in Czechoslovakia as well as in Cuba, and all but succeeded in seizing control of the country. The CIA, however, realized what was at stake and not wanting another Soviet-controlled country in their vicinity, sent the US Marines to put down the revolution.

Gradually Castro's attitude to the Russians became very cool and it was only through strong economic pressures being brought to bear by Moscow that he was forced to toe their line. Once this had been achieved the Soviet 'advisers' conducted a purge of the DGI. The director, Pineiro Losada, and all anti-Soviet personnel were transferred to the DLN which was made an independent organization without any kind of Soviet aid or advice. The KGB was only interested in running an Intelligence Service which would work for Moscow.

KGB Colonel Simenov took charge of the re-shuffle and placed José Mendez Cominches, a pro-Soviet officer at the head of the DGI. In addition, Cuban agents were sent to the Soviet Union to undergo training at the KGB/GRU spy schools.

Unlike the CIA which fled from Egypt when things began to go wrong, the KGB has no intention of leaving Cuba even if Castro does occasionally go his own way; they have far too much to lose to abandon it completely.

One of the most intriguing departments in Moscow is the 'Disinformation' section of the KGB. Its prime task is the dissemination of false rumours and misleading information. In 1968 this section carried out a concentrated campaign against the BBC and several Fleet Street journalists, accusing

Map showing location of the main KGB/GRU 'spy schools' and training centres.

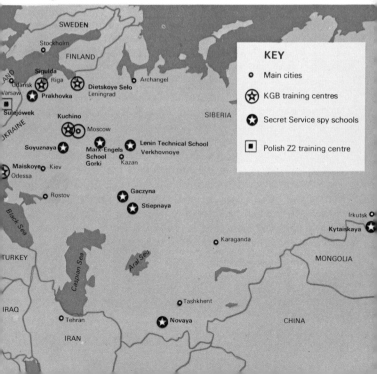

them of being agents of British Intelligence. In a long series of articles the Soviet press described how the BBC played certain tunes during their broadcasts to Russia as secret signals to agents in the Soviet Union. It was claimed that the BBC has a written agreement with DI6 to relay such messages over the air, contact between the two organizations allegedly being maintained through the British equivalent of the Department of Disinformation known as PROP-II. This musical method of contact was used for identification purposes. If a British agent in Russia wanted to prove his identity to a likely recruit he had only to arrange for a certain tune to be played on the BBC at a pre-arranged time. The KGB claimed that this proved that the agent was in contact with DI6 via the BBC.

A few days later the KGB tried to prove that the 'Freedom of the British Press' was nothing but a myth and that DI6 directed what went on in Fleet Street. If these accusations were to be believed the newspaper world in Britain is dominated by a mysterious British Intelligence department known, to the Russians anyway, as Z-I with its agents operating under the cover of journalists. Each of these agents has a code number beginning with the letters BIN, for example, Lord Arran of the 'Daily Mail' is referred to as BIN-1153, and Michael Berry of the 'Daily Telegraph' as BIN-943.

In 1971, agents of Department 'D' travelled around Europe in another attempt to discredit British Intelligence and to destroy the confidence of the Allied Secret Services in DI6; at the same time they began a smear campaign against the French SDECE to coincide with Mr Brezhnev's visit to Paris.

During the same year a 'purge' of Soviet agents took place in London. No less than 105 employees of the Russian government were ordered to return home by the British Foreign Office. For some years the staffs of the Soviet Embassy and Trade Mission had been steadily increasing out of all proportion to the diplomatic duties involved, and it was painfully obvious that the majority were engaged in activities other

(*Opposite*) Diagram showing the development of the Soviet Secret Service from its inception in 1917 to the present day, showing the many changes of name it has undergone during its history.

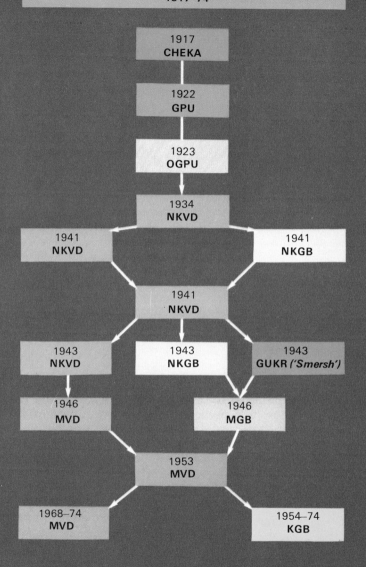

DEVELOPMENT OF THE SOVIET SECRET SERVICE
1917–74

1917
CHEKA

1922
GPU

1923
OGPU

1934
NKVD

1941
NKVD

1941
NKGB

1941
NKVD

1943
NKVD

1943
NKGB

1943
GUKR *('Smersh')*

1946
MVD

1946
MGB

1953
MVD

1968–74
MVD

1954–74
KGB

KGB Colonel Rudolf Abel, Soviet 'resident' agent in the US. After being exchanged he took over the training of Soviet agents at the Gaczyna spy school.

than their official ones. Department 'D' retaliated by stating that it was all the fault of Oleg Lyalin, a minor official at the Trade Mission in London who had defected shortly before the 'purge'. They maintained that DI5 had been completely misled by Lyalin, who the Russians considered as a minor defector, and that they had over-reacted as a result of his false information.

Over the years the Soviet Secret Service has changed its name several times. It was formed in 1917 as the CHEKA, which is the Russian abbreviation for the 'Extraordinary Commission to Combat Counter-Revolution, Sabotage and Subversion'. In 1922 it became the GPU (State Political Administration), and later the OGPU (United State Political Administration).

During the years of the Stalinist terror in the 1930s it was known as the NKVD (People's Commissariat for Internal Affairs) which became the most hated and feared secret police organization the world has ever known. It was the NKVD which carried out Stalin's purges, in the process of which they tortured thousands of Soviet citizens, murdered thousands more and sent several millions to their deaths in the slave labour camps of the Soviet far east and north.

There are no signs of any drastic changes taking place within the KGB at the time of writing, nor are there any signs of an easing of their espionage and terror-activities at home and abroad. It is an ever-present manifestation of a way of life and a mentality completely alien to the west.

Military Intelligence – GRU

The *GRU* was originally formed by Trotsky as the 4th Directorate of the General Staff of the Red Army. Its tasks and methods of operation are similar to those of the KGB, with the exception that most of its targets are of a military nature.

Military Intelligence headquarters is based at *Arbatskaya Ploshchad* in Moscow opposite the *Lubianka*, although it is almost certain that it also has offices in the main Ministry of Defence building. In 1947, the Russians attempted to centralize their Intelligence departments into a single agency. Known as KI, it was thought to be an attempt to emulate the newly-formed American CIA; the experiment failed and the idea was abandoned by the Kremlin.

Valentina Nikolayevna Malinovska alias 'Greta Nielsson', a Soviet agent trained at the Prakhovka spy school as a 'native' of Denmark where she was active for twelve years. 'Greta' was exposed by the Danish counter-espionage service but escaped before an arrest could be made. Her present whereabouts are unknown.

Microphone of the type planted by the KGB in Western Embassies in Moscow.

Almost all GRU agents are graduates of the Red Army Academy, an institution which not only provides military training for future officers, but also training in espionage techniques. In addition the GRU maintains several other training centres in and around Moscow.

Unlike the KGB, Soviet Military Intelligence does not publicly advertize its telephone numbers or the whereabouts of its offices.

'Smersh'

A great deal of misleading information exists about the special Intelligence units popularly known as *'Smersh'* immortalized in the James Bond stories.

Such a department did, in fact, exist, but was disbanded at the end of the Second World War, but was never the official murder-squad of the Soviet government as described by Ian Fleming.

Special units were established in 1921 within the Red Army, with the prime function of spying on the troops and removing any disloyal elements. They were known to the troops as the Double 'O' Detachments, the 'OO' referring to the Russian initials for their official name, *Osobyi Otdyel* (Special Section). The name 'Smersh' (an abbreviation for *Smiert Spionam* ('Death to Spies'), was not used until the Second World War. During this time its powers were extended to cover other counter-espionage activities and to set up its own courts with the right to deliver and execute sentences. Until 1946 *'Smersh'* was divided into several sub-sections, the main ones being Counter-espionage (DKR), Counter-intelligence (GUKR), and vetting and screening commissions (PFK).

At the end of the war all sections were absorbed into the Main Intelligence Administration and re-named the GUKR MGB. Through various administrative changes it gradually disappeared, its nearest counterpart today being the counter-intelligence section of the KGB.

Translation of a KGB card-index of a Soviet Intelligence agent.

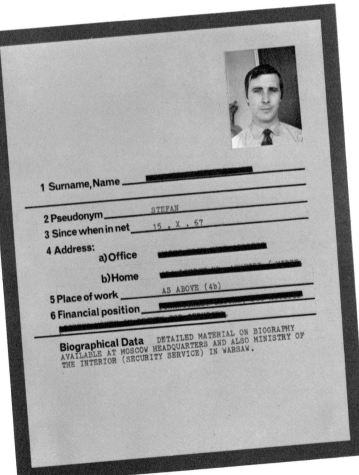

1 Surname, Name ▉▉▉▉▉▉▉▉▉▉▉▉▉

2 Pseudonym STEFAN
3 Since when in net 15 . X . 67

4 Address: a) Office ▉▉▉▉▉▉▉▉▉▉

b) Home ▉▉▉▉▉▉▉▉▉▉

5 Place of work AS ABOVE (4b)

6 Financial position ▉▉▉▉▉▉▉▉

▉▉▉▉▉▉▉▉▉▉▉▉▉▉

Biographical Data DETAILED MATERIAL ON BIOGRAPHY AVAILABLE AT MOSCOW HEADQUARTERS AND ALSO MINISTRY OF THE INTERIOR (SECURITY SERVICE) IN WARSAW.

EAST GERMANY

During the war two German communists met in Moscow and they were later instructed by the NKVD to draw up detailed plans for the formation of a Security Service for post-war Germany. Wilhelm Zaisser, who was given command of the proceedings, lacked the necessary qualifications for such a task and had to rely on the experience and information provided by a group of *Gestapo* and *Sicherheitsdienst* (SD – the Nazi élite Security Service) officers who were at that time being held in Soviet captivity. They were only too willing to assist in their new role as 'advisers'.

For the next three years this group dedicated themselves to evolving a system which was eventually put into effect in Saxony after the occupation by the Red Army. The Soviet authorities wanted to observe the effectiveness of the new Security apparatus on a local scale before deciding to expand it over the rest of the Zone of Occupation.

At first the Russians were reluctant to allow the East Germans to have a nation-wide secret police system of their own, but towards the end of 1945 new Government departments began to appear all over the Zone under the name of *'Kommissariat 5'* or *K5* as it came to be known.

Main entrance to the East German Ministry for State Security.

(*Left*) Lieutenant-Colonel Siegfried Dombrowski who defected from East German Intelligence; (*centre*) Wilhelm Zaisser and (*right*) Erich Mielke, founders and directors of the MfS/SSD.

K5 was nominally responsible for internal State Security, but for a 'probationary' period of two years its agents acted merely as 'assistants' to the Soviet Security forces which still refused to allow the formation of a central administrative agency. This state of affairs persisted until 1947 when K5 was finally accredited with legal powers of its own. But this was still not enough to combat the ever-increasing resistance to the 'Sovietization' of the East Zone, and it became necessary to form a second Security force which came to be known as the SSD directed by Erich Mielke, who was responsible for originally organizing K5 in its embryo form in Moscow with Zaisser. In 1950 the two organizations were amalgamated and moved into a central headquarters building at 22 Normannen-strasse, Berlin-Lichtenberg. K5 was officially disbanded and the new organization was named the *Ministry for State Security* (MfS) which, since its formation has expanded considerably several times. One of the most important additions has been that of a foreign Intelligence Service, known as the *Main Intelligence Administration* (HVA) directed by Marcus Wolf. This department performs the tasks of espionage abroad from a building on Gross-Berliner Damm in Berlin-Johannisthal; its main target being West Germany, but more recently its agents have been paying particular attention to the Scandinavian countries.

Prominent among the departments of the MfS is the 'Transport Section' which is a euphemism for the section specialising in political kidnapping and terror activities in West Berlin and the Federal Republic. Typical of the activities of this department is the case of Dr Walter Linse, a member of the Union of Free Jurists, an organization set up in 1949 to combat by legal means the gross violations of legality and principles of freedom in East Germany. All members of the UFJ were made fully aware of the dangerous nature of the work involved which would make them prime targets for the SSD.

Linse devoted himself to this work for three years until one morning in West Berlin as he was walking to work, a man asked him for a light in the street. As he reached into his pocket he was grabbed by the neck. Linse managed to fight-off his attacker and ran towards a taxi parked a few yards down the street. As he reached it he was grabbed and quickly bundled into the back seat. The taxi raced off with Linse's legs hanging out of the open door, the SSD agents shooting him in both legs in an attempt to get him inside.

The whole incident had been observed by another driver who immediately tried to ram the kidnap car. His attempts, however, were foiled by steel spikes strewn along the road by the fleeing kidnap-squad and by gunfire from the rear window. A West Berlin police patrol car joined the chase and as the East/West sector boundary was reached the barrier was immediately raised by the East German police to allow the kidnap-squad to dash through without stopping. The taxi disappeared into the Russian Sector.

Dr Walter Linse was next heard of in Vladamir prison in the Soviet Union several months later. In the meantime he had been interrogated under torture by the SSD and KGB and had broken-down and betrayed several East Germans who had been of assistance to the UFJ.

Linse's wife appealed to the Soviet authorities for the release of her husband. Her letter remained unanswered. She sent a food parcel to him at Vladamir prison which was returned marked 'address unknown'. Nothing has been heard of Dr Walter Linse since.

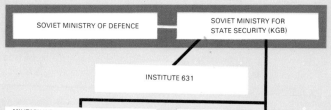

EAST GERMAN INTELLIGENCE SERVICES

| SOVIET MINISTRY OF DEFENCE | SOVIET MINISTRY FOR STATE SECURITY (KGB) |

INSTITUTE 631

MILITARY INTELLIGENCE SERVICE
ADMINISTRATION FOR CO ORDINATION
(Formerly Administration 19)

DIVISION A

TACTICAL INTELLIGENCE DEPARTMENT

WEST GERMAN MILITARY UNITS AND BASES

WEST GERMAN POLICE:
CITY, COUNTY, RIOT AND BORDER

NATO UNITS AND BASES

MILITARY UNITS AND
BASES OF OTHER COUNTRIES

DIVISION C

STRATEGIC INTELLIGENCE DEPARTMENT

ARMAMENTS,
WEAPONS DEVELOPMENT

NATO TROOPS

GREAT BRITAIN

FRANCE

BELGIUM

NETHERLANDS

SCANDINAVIA

LUXEMBURG

DENMARK

ITALY

SPAIN

AIR AND NAVAL FORCES

DIVISION T

SECRET WEAPONS DEPARTMENT

STRATEGIC DEVICES

ARMAMENTS FACTORIES AND SUPPLIES

CHEMICAL PLANTS

MINISTRY FOR STATE SECURITY *(MfS)*
STATE SECURITY SERVICE (SSD)
(Formerly K5)

DEPARTMENT I

DEPARTMENT II

COUNTER-INTELLIGENCE

SECTION I
Against U.S. Intelligence
SECTION II
Against British Intelligence
SECTION III
Against French Intelligence
SECTION IV
Against W. German Intelligence
SECTION V
Against Refugee Organizations in W. Europe

19 other departments engaged in transport,
kidnapping, radio communications,
codes and ciphers

DEPARTMENT K

TECHNICAL WORKSHOPS DEPARTMENT

ELECTRONICS

PHOTOGRAPHY

FORGED DOCUMENTS

The MfS/KGB complex in East Berlin runs another highly successful department which, at times, has created untold havoc in West Germany. Known as *Institute 631*, based in Berlin-Pankow, it deals with forgery of a remarkably high standard. So high in fact that some of its documents have remained undetected for a long time.

One of its most successful operations almost brought the West German armed forces to a standstill. The expert printers of Pankow produced vast quantities of conscription and demobilization documents and sent them to the male population of West Germany of the appropriate age groups. The armed forces administration all but collapsed under the strain of trying to penetrate the ensuing chaos; thousands of young men turning up unexpectedly at military camps with seemingly genuine call-up papers and thousands of regular troops who simply went home, believing they had been demobilized.

Counterfeit currency of various types, of a very high quality, is also produced and distributed by Institute 631. That such notes existed was only discovered when the West German clearing banks noticed recurring serial numbers on large amounts of money. Experts were consulted but even they could not distinguish which was the genuine article and which was the craftmanship of the printers in Pankow.

East German Military Intelligence (VfK)

East German Military Intelligence was set up in 1953 as a separate organization from the MfS. Originally known as *Administration 19*, under the directorship of Karl Linke, it operated until 1957 from No. 42–45 Behrens-Strasse in East Berlin.

Unfortunately for Linke he was accused in 1957 of 'losing official documents' and promptly lost his post. In the same year *Administration 19*, since renamed the VfK, moved to new premises at 25–29 Regatta-Strasse, Berlin-Grünau, with a new director, Willi Sägebrecht. One of his three deputies, Siegfried Dombrowski, defected in August 1958, bringing with him invaluable information on the Soviet, East German and other East bloc Intelligence Services. Dombrowski, like his directors, had been Moscow trained and recruited in 1955, and placed in charge of a VfK department. Unknown to his masters, he had met an agent who had a double-role with the West German BfV and American CIA. Dombrowski agreed to provide information to the West on VfK personnel, methods and duties, and the rivalries existing between his Service and the MfS/SSD.

For two years West German Intelligence received a constant flow of information. Then, it was discovered that the KGB suspected a high-ranking agent in the ranks of the VfK was passing information to the West. It could only be Dombrowski. A combined effort by the KGB and SSD confirmed their suspicions but before any drastic action could be taken Dombrowski fled to the West, bringing with him a vast amount of photostat copies of KBG/VfK and MfS documents.

This was the chance the rival SSD had been waiting for. A ruthless purge was carried-out in which Linke lost his job, and together with sixty-nine other officers was arrested by the SSD. Another two hundred men were summarily dismissed from the Service. It took the VfK five years to recover from the damage inflicted by Dombrowski and the resulting purge.

MfS/SSD headquarters, Normannenstrasse, East Berlin. (*Inset*)
Dr. Walter Linse, victim of an SSD 'kidnap squad'.

POLAND

Z-2 – Military Intelligence

Polish Military Intelligence, known as Z-2, has its headquarters in a large, grim, fortress-like building on Niepodległóśći Avenue in Warsaw. All the windows on the ground and first floors – and many as high as the fifth – are heavily barred. Armed guards surround the building day and night; even with a pass a visitor must be accompanied by an official escort to gain entry. Special passes are required to take any kind of document-case in or out. There are two separate security checks inside the building for regular employees of Z-2; entry is through three massive metal doors along the front of the building, only one being used at a time.

One section is occupied by the Reports and Evaluation Department. Here, trained analysts read, compile and elaborate on reports received concerning the defence installations of the West. Vast piles of technical and scientific periodicals from all over the world are read and any interesting items evaluated and filed.

On another floor is located the 'Wardrobe Department', in which is kept all the apparel from various countries used to outfit an agent being sent abroad.

The Technical Section, where all the gadgetry of espionage is produced, was for many years located in a villa on Wawelska Street, a quiet, side-turning off Niepodległóśći Avenue. More recent reports now locate this section as being in Bielany, a residential quarter of north Warsaw. During the Gomułka régime (1956–70) the head of Military Intelligence was Janusz Lipiański.

The agents of Z-2 are trained on an estate at Sulejówek, about ten miles east of Warsaw. During the war General Gehlen, ex-director of West German Intelligence, used the same location for his Eastern Front Intelligence HQ. Training courses are intensive, embracing all the techniques used by agents in the field. Special sessions are held to see how the agents would react under pressure, which have been reported to be 'rather severe'.

According to information supplied by Z-2 defectors, one of the functions of the Sulejówek school is the training of agents

Plain-clothed agents of the Polish SB and uniformed officers of the Internal Security Corps (WOW, formerly KBW).

to be planted at strategic spots in the West. Their task will be to prepare the way for Communist sabotage teams which will precede the armies of the Warsaw Pact in the event of a conventional war breaking-out. These teams belong to a special sabotage battalion modelled on the American Special Services forces, seconded to Z-2 for their orders and trained at a camp near Wrocław in Silesia (South West Poland).

Not a great deal is ever heard of Polish agents operating in the West. One operation which the Poles made sure we heard about by giving it the widest-possible publicity, once the agent was safely home in Warsaw, was carried out by Captain Andrzej Czechowicz. In 1965 he 'defected' and managed to outwit American counter-espionage during a long series of interrogations, and eventually penetrated Radio Free Europe in Munich, the CIA-backed anti-Communist radio station broadcasting to Eastern Europe. For seven years this agent passed a steady stream of information to Warsaw which resulted in the tracing and arrest of large numbers of informers and networks in Poland.

In 1971 he quietly returned to Warsaw and his exploits in West Germany were published in the Polish Press and broadcast on the radio. On 19 July 1973 he was quietly married in Warsaw; only a photograph with a six line caption appeared in one newspaper.

One of the most controversial agents ever to defect was Lieutenant Colonel Michał Goleniewski of Z-2. His case has turned-out to be the most complicated in the history of espionage.

For some years the CIA had been receiving information from an anonymous agent behind the Iron Curtain who called himself *'Heckenschütze'*. Certainly his information indicated that he was a high-ranking member of an Eastern-bloc Intelligence Service.

The first anyone in the West heard of Goleniewski was on Christmas Day, 1960, when he crossed into West Berlin and announced that he was *'Heckenschütze'* and wanted political asylum. Over the years this mystery agent had always insisted on dealing with the FBI and not the CIA. It came as a shock to him to discover that his information had been going to the CIA all along. He promptly claimed that several high-ranking CIA agents were working for the KGB. The information he poured out during his de-briefing was shattering and for the most part proved to be correct. But it meant that if acted upon large numbers of CIA and State Department personnel would lose their jobs, and an almost entirely new Intelligence Service would have to be formed. Needless to say no such drastic action was ever taken.

For some time after his defection Goleniewski continued to argue and quarrel with the CIA, insisting that the agents he had named were Soviet double-agents. Finally, seven years later, he announced that he was the son of the last Tsar of Russia and that the Imperial Romanov Family did not die at the hands of a Red execution squad!

To this day no-one really knows how much of his story is true. It is seriously doubted whether his real name is Goleniewski. Was he sent by the KGB/Z-2 to deliberately spread chaos and alarm about the extent of Soviet penetration in the West? Was the Romanov story added at a later date when things were already highly complicated – just to add more confusion? One thing is certain: 'Goleniewski' has certainly given Western Intelligence plenty to think about and they are no nearer to clearing-up the ramifications of his story than they were ten years ago. Perhaps the Russians and the Poles have perpetrated their greatest *coup* in the war of 'Disinformation'; they have certainly succeeded in completely confusing more than one Western Intelligence Service.

Adam Muller, a Polish-born American engineer before the Warsaw Military Court. Arrested in May 1971 while visiting his family in Poland he was accused of espionage and charged with passing information to British, American and French Intelligence. He was released after serving only one month of a five year sentence.

SB – Security Service

The Polish Security Service, the SB, (UB or *'Bezpieka'* as it is commonly called) is housed in the Ministry of the Interior, the MSW, a complex of buildings at No. 2 Rakowiecka Street, Warsaw. The building is in the shape of an 'E', the vertical line being parallel to Rakowiecka Street and housing the main administration departments. Behind this, hidden from public view, are blocks A, B and C, of which block A is the HQ of Polish Security. Here, the specialists in political and economic espionage and counter-espionage operate in strict secrecy. All non-essential documents are burnt after use; the doors are padded with leather and guarded by armed members of the Internal Security Corps. The names of the personnel employed here are unknown to the public – those that are known are assumed names.

Early in 1973 reports reached the west of a newly-formed department of the MSW in Warsaw called 'Bureau I-S'. This is apparently an independent section responsible only and directly to the head of the SB. Its powers are unlimited and it has been compared to a now defunct department which existed until 1971 known as Department *'one zero four'*, which seems to have been a surveillance section. I-S is concerned with 'political sabotage' in Poland and its functions sound very similar to the hated 10th Department of the Stalinist UB, which became notorious during the 1950s for its horrific methods of interrogation under Józef Swiatło who defected in 1953. The director of I-S is reported to be an officer from Z-2 whose name is at present unknown. One of the notable changes which he had brought about is that the MSW/SB Intelligence representative in Polish Embassies abroad (usually the 2nd Councillor) has now been demoted and his place taken by a member of I-S.

A special SB Academy is known to exist in Bielany, a northern suburb of Warsaw, with two subsidiaries, one at Legionowo, a few miles north of the city, and the other near Katowice in Silesia. Few details are known about these training establishments, only the name of the Director at Bielany, Colonel Marian Lipka. His deputies are unknown.

For many years a name which kept cropping up in Security matters was that of General Mieczysław Moczar, an ex-partisan leader and veteran Security official. He began his career as security chief in the town of Łódź in central Poland, where he became notorious for the ruthless methods he used in liquidating the bands of anti-communist partisans which roamed the countryside in the post-war years. In the mid-1960s Moczar was Deputy Minister of the Interior and he eventually became chief of the SB.

Under Moczar the SB seemed in danger of becoming once more an instrument of terror. In 1968 he precipitated a violent anti-Zionist campaign which got out of hand and resulted in 'excesses of legality' which brought about his removal from SB affairs.

Since 1970 the SB has had three different directors in quick succession, one of them being killed in a plane crash together with the head of Czech Security in March 1973. It was announced from Warsaw that May that a certain Stanisław Kowalczyk had been appointed as the new head of Polish Security.

(*Left*) Michał Goleniewski, defector from Z2, Polish Military Intelligence. (*Right*) Mieczysław Moczar, veteran Polish Security Service official and former head of the Secret Police (SB).

COMMUNIST CHINA

Number 15, Bow String Alley in Peking is a large but unimpressive building bearing the innocuous-sounding name of Department for Social Affairs, but in spite of its name, the offices of this department have nothing whatever to do with the social welfare of the citizens of the Chinese Peoples' Republic. It is in fact the headquarters of the Communist Chinese Intelligence and Security Services, formerly directed by K'ang Sheng, who had the unique position of being in control of both Foreign Intelligence and Internal Security.

Far from hiding in the political shadows like most Intelligence chiefs K'ang occasionally appeared at various functions abroad as the representative of Mao's government. In the mid-1950s he visited East Berlin as chief Chinese delegate at the Third Congress of Socialist Party Unity, and later turned-up in Moscow with Chou En-lai to attend the Twenty-First Congress of the Communist Party of the Soviet Union.

It was K'ang who first directed an official verbal attack on the Russians in the then steadily-growing Sino-Soviet dispute. Prior to this the differences of political opinion had been a more diplomatic, gentlemanly affair, restricted to criticisms of their Soviet comrades veiled in the ponderous language of Marxist dialectic. Things were never the same after K'ang's fiery outbursts, which continued from then on. At about the same time the irascible old Intelligence chief adopted a very tough policy towards the West, and the United States in particular.

Chinese espionage abroad is mainly directed from two other departments which also have rather innocent-sounding names: the United Front Workers' Department and the International Liaison Department. The former agency maintains strong links abroad with the several million Chinese who have taken-up permanent residence in various countries around the world, and utilizes many of them for espionage activities. In addition it also endeavours to persuade as many of these ethnic Chinese as possible to return to their Motherland.

As is the case with most other countries China uses its embassies fully as diplomatic cover for espionage activities. In some cases Trade or Cultural Missions are used for the same purposes; the New China News Agency, for example, is in reality merely a 'front' for Intelligence and subversive activities. The classic example of this occurred in 1965 when the Arab Communist Party, which is very much pro-Peking, was involved in an attempt to assassinate the late President Nasser. During the ensuing investigation by the Egyptian Security Service it was established that a link existed between the would-be assassins and the Chinese Embassy in Cairo. The ambassador hurriedly left the country immediately this was made known, to be followed very soon afterwards by the director of the New China News Agency. Egyptian Security officials accused him of financing the murder plot.

More than fifty countries around the world have New China News Agency offices on their territory, the largest single contingent being in Hong Kong, where over one hundred 'journalists' are posted. Oddly enough, they rarely seem to attend any press conferences or frequent any of the numerous journalists' clubs. One of the few countries which refuses to have an agency office is Czechoslovakia, which expelled the entire staff in 1963 for 'biased reporting'.

Red Chinese agents are trained in spy schools which closely resemble those of the Soviet KGB/GRU. Stalin realized as early as the 1920s that China would inevitably turn to Communism and consequently gave orders for the training of Chinese agents in the Soviet Union. The first such establishment was at Kytaiskaya, and it recruited personnel from students who had been sent to the Lenin School. By the early 1930s Kytaiskaya had produced about three hundred fully trained Chinese agents.

When Mao Tse-tung had finally established his government the Chinese organized their own Intelligence Service in Peking, using the knowledge gained by their Soviet-trained agents. They soon realized, however, that they were still not capable of running a large espionage apparatus on their own, and had to rely on Soviet 'technical advisers' lent by Stalin. These advisers were in effective control of Chinese Intelligence during its early formative years.

Before long Mao established his own schools and training centres, although 'students' were still being sent to the Soviet Union until the 'idealogical differences' between Soviet and

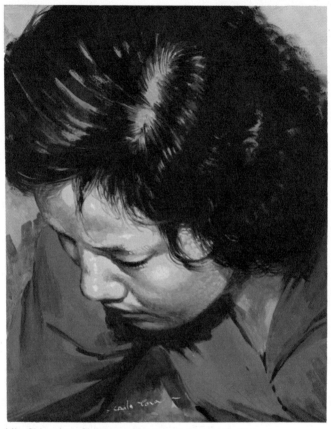

Min Chiau-sen, Chinese resident agent in the US. She was murdered in mysterious circumstances in New York.

Chinese communism became pronounced during the Khrushchev régime. From that time on all Chinese agents were trained in their own centres.

There are few countries which have not been infiltrated by the Ministry of Social Affairs or its two related departments. Latest reports indicate that the Chinese are conducting an extensive 'undercover' war against the non-communist countries and their successes have shown that they are equally as efficient and deadly as their former masters in Moscow. There seems to be an ever-increasing number of agents in the employ of Peking who are not Chinese nationals but fifth columnists and fellow-travellers who are not known to the Security Services of their countries as being communists. As they are not 'blacklisted' or under any form of surveillance for suspect activities they have little difficulty in infiltrating any organization or department which Peking has an interest in.

China's number one target is, and always has been, Hong Kong, and the lists of agents arrested by British counter-espionage officers in this port are staggering in length. Vast dossiers are kept of all known infiltrators, agitators and agents, and the security problem there has reached such tremendous proportions that little information is released officially.

Chinese counter-espionage and internal security, also formerly directed by K'ang, is the concern of the Ministry of Public Affairs, which deals not only with the Chinese mainland, but also Hong Kong, Taiwan and Macao. Its numerical strength has been estimated by American Intelligence at approximately 250,000 police and agents who in turn control a vast network of informers. The deputy director under K'ang of this mammoth security apparatus was political commissar Hsieh Fu-chih, who made a name for himself for being violently anti-Japanese and anti-Chiang Kai-shek.

K'ang Sheng, former head of Chinese Intelligence. He was one of the few Intelligence chiefs who did not shun publicity, unlike many of his Western counterparts. He still receives quite extensive publicity in the Chinese Press.

One of K'ang's most successful agents operating abroad was Min Chiau-sen who worked under the name of 'Lily Petal' as Resident Agent in the United States for many years. Her activities only came to light during a routine murder enquiry in 1969 by the New York Homicide Squad.

The bodies of two Chinese, later identified as Lily Petal and Wang En-ping, were discovered in a chop-suey restaurant on New York's waterfront. After an investigation lasting several months, the affair petered out and went on record as just one more of the city's many unsolved murders. It does the Chinese Intelligence Service credit that in spite of the massive police investigation involving several departments, it was not discovered at the time that the restaurant had been for the past fifteen years the Headquarters of Chinese Intelligence in the US with Lily Petal as its director. Neither was it discovered then that the dead woman was not the real Lily Petal. It was only through an event which occurred some three weeks before her death that the story eventually came to light, and even then not the full background to 'Lily Petal's' career.

Sixteen years before the murder, the real Lily Petal, an American citizen from Chicago of Chinese descent, embarked on a visit to her homeland. Somewhere off the Chinese Mainland the boat on which she was travelling sank, her body being recovered by a Red Chinese patrol boat. The normal procedure in similar events was for the Communists to forward the passport and other relevant details to the British authorities in Hong Kong. This was never done. Lily Petal's American passport eventually ended up in the Ministry of Social Affairs where a newly-trained female agent was about to be sent to the United States as Resident Operator, and the passport provided a perfect cover and background for this agent, Min Chiau-sen.

After a brief stop in Hong Kong to deliver a tale of woe to the British counter-espionage authorities about her capture and release by the Red Chinese, 'Lily Petal' made her way to New York. Once established on American soil she opened a chop-suey restaurant which provided the cover needed to explain the comings and goings of her network of agents.

For some time all went well. Then the resident Soviet agent

discovered 'Lily Petal's' real occupation. He promptly informed the KGB in Moscow explaining the potential of this Chinese agent and a reply was soon forthcoming with instructions to recruit her. This was duly carried out with the help of Colonel Rudolf Abel, one of the most successful Soviet agents ever to operate in the United States. For several years 'Lily Petal' fulfilled the role of a 'double agent' completely undetected by the FBI.

She remained active for her Chinese and Russian masters until the day a visitor called at the restaurant demanding to see Lily Petal. The one event she had dreaded for fifteen years – a confrontation with a friend of the real Lily Petal. There was only one course open to her: disappear and re-emerge in China.

Unfortunately her masters in Peking noted her sudden disappearance and wrongly concluded that their number one agent had defected. A special squad from the Operations Division was dispatched to New York with orders to find and liquidate her.

Three weeks later she was found stabbed to death.

Chinese microfilm and key-codes.

TECHNOLOGY

Espionage by technology is a vast, complicated subject with gadgets and equipment ranging from the well-known Minox camera pictured opposite and the 4-inch square radio transmitter on page 100, to supersonic jets which flash across another country's airspace photographing military installations. Certain electronic devices may also be used for counter-intelligence purposes as they were by the KGB against the American Embassy in Moscow.

During the 1960s American Security agents discovered strange micro-wave impulses being beamed at the US Embassy from a nearby building. Details of the waves were supplied to American military scientists who carried out micro-wave radiation tests on monkeys for several months in an attempt to discover exactly what the Russians were trying to do.

Meanwhile, the CIA had learned that Soviet scientists had hinted that such micro-waves were capable of causing irritability, nervous tension and nervous disorders. From this US Intelligence speculated that the KGB could well be conducting experiments in an attempt to drive American diplomats insane. The tests carried out in the USA in a project code-named 'Operation Pandora', using similar techniques, concluded that there was no proof that low-level radiation as used in Moscow was particularly harmful.

It has never been fully established just what the KGB hoped

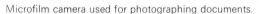

Microfilm camera used for photographing documents.

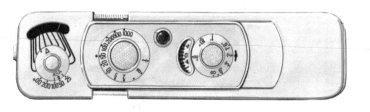

(*Above*) Minox camera and (*below*) the orthodox method of photographing documents.

to achieve; another theory put forward was that they were using the micro-waves as a sophisticated new surveillance technique in which conversations could be overheard through the bending of the waves by voices in the US Embassy.

If this strange episode were indeed an experiment in eaves-dropping it was rather primitive compared with a device

introduced in the early 1970s. Known as the 'Infinity Bug', it enables a private telephone to be used for picking up conversations in any part of the world. Officially known as the Monitel Mark II this apparatus can monitor conversations in any other country providing that it is possible to dial directly the telephone at the other end. In spite of its tremendous scope and range the bug is quite small enabling it to be easily concealed and has the added advantage of not requiring a separate power supply. Its applications, according to the makers, are limited only by the imagination of its user.

Technological espionage has, to a large extent, dispensed with the need for agents to infiltrate into other countries, but by no means entirely superseded them. The most famous examples of electronic Intelligence gathering are the U2 spy flights but these have long since been replaced by more advanced spy planes such as the EC-121, the A-11 and the SR-71.

Occasional unrevealing photographs of the SR-71 have been released from time to time by US military censors, but certain details of its performance and functions are now known. Flying at speeds of 2,000 mph 120,000 feet up on the edge of

Four-inch-square radio transmitter found on an agent by the Polish counter-espionage service.

American SR-71 spy plane, successor to the U2.

the earth's atmosphere this super-spy in the sky can produce telephoto close-ups in black and white or grainless colour shots of the territory being overflown, usually Red China and until recently, North Vietnam. It is also equipped with 'side-looking' radar which maps the terrain for great distances on either side of the flight-path. It has also been rumoured that when ground radar picks-up its course an automatic device gives it 'electronic invisibility'; this, coupled with its speed and high altitude make it almost invulnerable. At the moment it is the next best thing to a manned orbiting satellite.

The first Satellite and Missile Observation System (SAMOS) was launched twelve years ago and was capable of picking up radio signals from the ground and taking photographs of selected military targets from a height of 150 miles. The Intelligence collected was ejected at regular intervals into the Pacific Ocean where it was retrieved by ships of the National Security Agency.

Soviet spy aircraft are also much in evidence over and around Western Europe, eavesdropping on NATO communications, taking photographs and testing the alertness of the various air forces which periodically send up planes to warn them off.

At the time of the capture of the US spy ship *Pueblo* the Americans had fifteen such ships, known as the Electronic Intelligence Fleet (ELINT), patrolling the oceans of the world. From the safety of international waters they can pinpoint the precise locations of radio transmitters as well as intercept all radio and telephone messages and conversations. The Russians also have their 'floating spy stations' concealed within its ocean-going trawling fleet. Large numbers of these ships are known to double as electronic surveillance bases; they always appear in force whenever any kind of NATO naval activity takes place, shadowing the Allied warships.

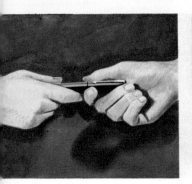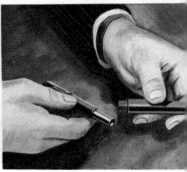

A weapon used by the KGB 'murder-squads'. Twisting the cap of the pen fires a .22 bullet.

Murder Weapons

An interesting device fell into the hands of West German Intelligence in 1954 when Captain Nikolai Khokhlov of the Soviet Secret Service defected while on an assassination assignment. This KGB officer divulged during interrogations that he was a member of the Ninth Section for Diversion and Terror and had been sent to Frankfurt with orders to liquidate Georgi Okolovich, leader of the NTS, an anti-communist Russian organisation based in France.

Khokhlov, upon arriving in West Germany, immediately confessed to his intended victim and asked for political asylum. In the weeks that followed he divulged all he knew about the KGB murder squads and admitted that he was himself a trained killer and had carried out several successful 'assignments' on the instructions of his superiors in Moscow.

The weapon provided to silence Okolovich caused a sensation and was given the widest possible publicity. It was a specially constructed dummy cigarette case, a product of the KGB training centre at Kuchino near Moscow. Powered by small batteries it fired special bullets which had been treated with potassium cyanide.

Another KGB-produced gadget, a silent poison-gas pistol, came to light in 1961 when Bogdan Stashinsky, also a Soviet trained professional assassin, gave himself up in West Berlin. At first the German CID refused to believe his incredible stories of the murder missions he had accomplished in their country.

Some years before two violently anti-communist Ukranian nationalists had died in Munich, supposedly from heart attacks, but according to Stashinsky he had murdered them on orders from Moscow. Realizing that his revelations were not being taken seriously, he demanded to be handed over to the Americans. For several weeks officers of the American CIC (Counter-Intelligence Corps) checked his story before passing him on to the BfV. His confession was proved to be one hundred per cent accurate.

The murders had been committed with a special gas gun which fired glass capsules containing hydrocyanic acid. When fired directly at the face of the victim the capsules broke releasing their deadly load of poison gas which paralysed the heart. The gas very quickly dispersed leaving no trace, the victim showing every sign of having suffered a heart seizure. The assassin was not affected having taken an anti-poison capsule immediately before releasing the gas.

Specially-constructed cigarette case issued to KGB captain Nikolai Khokhlov. When the victim attempts to remove a cigarette a trigger mechanism fires poisoned bullets.

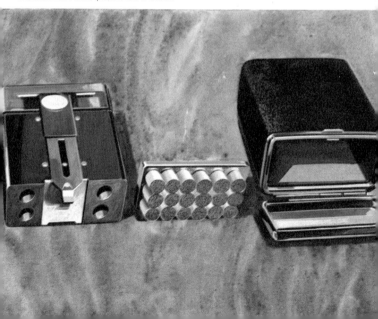

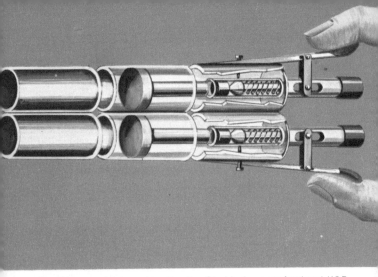

Cyanide gas-pistol used by Bogdan Stashinsky, a professional KGB killer. He received training in the Soviet Union in the use of specially-constructed murder weapons before being sent to West Germany on 'assignments'. There he liquidated two leaders of an anti-communist organization based in Munich. After carrying-out his murder-missions successfully he returned to the Soviet Union but later defected.

(*Left*) Bogdan Stashinsky the KGB assassin and Stefan Bandera (*right*) one of his victims.

CODES AND CIPHERS

In the present age of telecommunications codes and ciphers have become a secret industry throughout the world, while the breaking of codes has become the most important form of Intelligence for any Secret Service; every espionage and security organization relies heavily on its communications sections where codes and ciphers are in constant use.

The two largest agencies in the world belong, of course, to the Soviet Union and the United States, both of which employ several thousand cryptanalytical experts whose sole task is the making and breaking of codes and ciphers using the most sophisticated electronic techniques available, including computers.

No spy can operate efficiently and expect to escape detection without employing some form of secret communication which is unintelligible to the opposition. These may range from a coded radio-transmission sent at high speed, the whole transmission taking only seconds; to the type of code book illustrated below. Known as a 'one time pad' and used

Examples of different types of codes and ciphers. (*Left*) code book shown actual size. (*Inset*) microdots, actual size.

extensively by Soviet agents, it can take several forms, the most common being the one shown; alternatively, it may be in scroll form, no bigger than a cigarette filter. The printing is usually in two colours, black and red, one for coding and the other decoding. As the name suggests, these pads are used only once and the codes are virtually unbreakable.

In Iran, counter-espionage agents captured a KGB cipher in the form of what appeared to be trigometric equations, but mathematically the formulae were nonsense. It took two cryptanalysts working twenty four hours a day in twelve hour shifts three days to crack the cipher which the captured agent had insisted was unbreakable.

Responsibility for US cryptology and cryptanalysis lies with the National Security Agency (NSA), without doubt the biggest and most secret Intelligence department in the world. Even the presidential directive which brought it into being in 1952 is still classified and for five years the very existence of the NSA was never mentioned publicly.

The nerve-centre of this super-secret organization is the Office for Research and Development (R/D) which is divided into three main sections. One deals with foreign cryptosystems,

Electric coding machine.

Two hiding places for microfilm.

attempting to crack them by applying statistics, higher algebra and computers. Another produces new forms of encipherment, occasionally using rather bizarre methods; and the third carries out transmission research, aimed at increasing the sensitivity of US Intelligence receivers and improving the security of methods of transmission using the extreme limits of radio frequencies.

COMSEC (Communications Security) is the only NSA department which is officially acknowledged to exist. Here, the technicians are responsible for the protection of US government communications and providing the machinery used for encoding and enciphering government messages. During 1968 it was believed that this department also provided such machines for British government, military and diplomatic departments. As the Americans have admitted that they had read all the codes which passed between the British and French at the time of the Suez invasion, and it is almost certain that they have supplied the necessary machines since the end of the war, it would seem reasonable to assume that no British coded message is a secret to American Intelligence.

SPY EXCHANGES

A common feature of the underworld of espionage over the past fifteen years has been exchanges between East and West of 'blown' agents and in some recent cases of a political nature, hostages. Such classic cases as Colonel Rudolf Abel, Gary Powers and Gordon Lonsdale are well-known but the extent of this barter in human lives (and occasionally dead bodies) is not generally known. It has quietly and steadily become an almost unwritten law among Intelligence Agencies that important agents can expect to be exchanged and returned home within a comparatively short time of their arrest. Unfortunately most of the advantages in this behind-the-scenes trade seem to be gained by the Communists.

It is no longer true that an agent arrested with all his equipment, interrogated at length by the Security Service of either side and eventually imprisoned, is no longer of any use to his directors. Although the Intelligence gathered during his term of operation may be long out of date by the time he is exchanged, it is still vital for his department to learn what went wrong, and the methods used by the opposing counter-espionage service to detect his actions. Useful information may be gleaned during the de-briefing of a returned agent of the interrogation methods used against

Dr. Wolfgang Vogel (*left*) the spy-exchange lawyer.

(*Above left*) KGB Colonel Molody, better known as Gordon Lonsdale, and (*above right*) Helen and Peter Kroger, arrested for their part in the Portland spy ring and later exchanged. Lonsdale was exchanged for Greville Wynne and the Krogers for Gerald Brooke, both being held by the Russians on charges of espionage.

(*Below left*) Valentin Pripoltzev, KGB resident director in West Germany, exchanged for four Germans accused of spying in Russia. (*Below right*) Irena Schultz, a communist agent who was employed as personal secretary to the West German Minister of Technology. Vogel began negotiations for her exchange immediately after her arrest.

him. This has proved to be the case with both Abel and Lonsdale who returned to the Soviet Union with first-hand accounts of Western counter-espionage methods which they put to good use in training KGB/GRU agents at Soviet spy schools.

Most of this trade in agents has been conducted by Wolfgang Vogel, an East German lawyer whose name began to appear more and more frequently during the numerous exchanges carried out during the mid-1960s. His first big case was the Abel/Powers exchange in 1962. Since then he has acted as intermediary in dozens of cases, many of them still secret.

Vogel lives and works in a large villa in East Berlin at 4 Reilerstrasse, where he employs half a dozen secretaries and several lawyers as partners in his strange dealings in human lives. He only handles the most important exchanges personally.

In East Germany his professional position and personal status is almost unique. Since 1954 he has been one of a handful of lawyers in East Germany who have been allowed to function independently of the Ministry of Justice, and is one of only two East German lawyers admitted to the West German bar. He possesses a rare document issued by the four powers occupying Berlin which enables him to cross the East/West border whenever he chooses, a rare privilege enjoyed by very few East Germans.

Between 1965 and 1970 he was kept constantly busy negotiating exchanges. Some of them made the international headlines, most are still known only to the Secret Services of the West and the KGB.

In 1969 occurred what must be his most bizarre case to date: the exchange of an East German corpse for two West Germans held by the SSD. For some time the West Berlin police had been trying to establish the identity of a woman killed by a taxi on the Kantstrasse. She apparently carried no documents on her person, only a telephone number. On checking this number police learned that the owner had picked her up one night in Berlin, that she claimed to be a teacher from Hanover, and that her name was Ute Schwartz. A passport in this name was later found in the dead woman's flat. Ute Schwartz, however, was soon discovered to be still very much

Greville Wynne, the British businessman arrested for espionage in Russia, pictured before his arrest by the KGB (*inset*) and after his release from Soviet captivity. Wynne acted as a go-between for Colonel Oleg Penkovsky of the GRU who was probably the most valuable agent ever to pass information to the West. On his last mission, to bring Penkovsky out to the West, Wynne was arrested. After serving part of his sentence he was exchanged for Gordon Lonsdale.

East/West exchange point, Heerstrasse, Berlin.

alive in Hanover, still had her passport and had never been to Berlin.

A thorough search was made of the mystery woman's flat during which several ciphers were found together with a list of East German addresses. The case was promptly handed over to the West German BfV. Photographs were circulated of the woman until one day a letter arrived from East Germany identifying her as Gudrun Heidel and requesting the return of the body to her family.

No explanation was ever forthcoming for her assumed identity or what she was doing in West Berlin with a forged passport. The BfV assumed that she was an agent of the MfS, but no details were made public.

At this juncture the West German Government notified Vogel that the return of the body could be arranged only if two West Germans arrested some time previously in East

Germany were to be released and exchanged. Vogel clinched the deal successfully; perhaps to the advantage of the West for a change.

The most classic case of how the East nearly always seems to get the better part of the bargain is that of Alfred Frenzel, a member of the West German *Bundestag* who betrayed NATO defence secrets to the Czech SNB. He was arrested in 1960 and accused of having passed information over a period of at least four years. On the surface Frenzel appeared to make a full and detailed confession of his activities with Czechoslovak Intelligence, and it was only much later that the BfV realised that everything he had said was a cleverly devised series of lies. He was given a fifteen year sentence.

The traitor had only been in prison a very short time when both the Soviet and Czech Governments attempted to obtain his release. Meanwhile the BfV had been investigating his past and discovered that in his youth he had been an active communist and later entered West German politics and finally the Establishment. When approached by comrades from former days he was only too eager to oblige with information which he duly passed to the Czech SNB.

Due to the efforts of Vogel, Frenzel was exchanged for a West German woman who, according to the Soviet authorities, had infringed the Russian travel regulations imposed on all foreigners in the Soviet Union. Frenzel duly disappeared into Czechoslovakia and nothing more was heard of him until his death was announced in 1969 from Prague.

(*Left*) Gudrun Heidel. (*Right*) Alfred Frenzel.

INDUSTRIAL INTELLIGENCE

Industrial Intelligence is a combination of the perfectly legal collection of information and industrial espionage, which is the illegal collection of data; it covers a wide field of activity ranging from comparative shopping to computer-tapping. Over the past twenty five years all types of trade have been infiltrated in most countries of the world, particularly in the United States, West Germany and France. It has not yet reached unmanageable proportions in Great Britain probably because the sale and use of bugging and surveillance devices is illegal.

As is the case with most national espionage agencies, industrial spies often operate under cover-names or euphemistically named businesses, the most common being 'management consultants' or 'management advisers'. For obvious reasons they do not advertise their presence and methods publicly and are as equally difficult to detect as the agents of a foreign power.

The easiest method of obtaining Industrial Intelligence is to pay a number of strategically-placed personnel a retaining fee in the hope that when information is required from those scources it is readily obtainable. At the other end of the scale information may only be obtained by breaking into premises and photographing whatever is required by the client. The

Miniature spy-camera which fits into a cigarette packet.

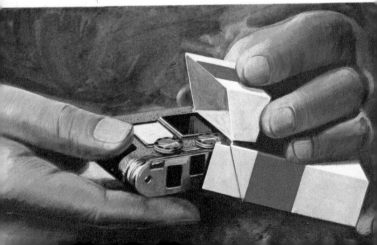

Shot-gun microphone which consists of a directional microphone inside a barrel which can be aimed at the sound-source in the same way as a gun.

same breaking-in method may also have to be used to install electronic listening devices to eavesdrop on conversations, meetings and telephone-calls, and which have the advantage of enabling the agent to obtain the information in comfort without any personal risk. Some of the more widely used equipment available for operations of this kind is illustrated in this chapter.

When one considers that bugging is illegal the prices listed are by no means exorbitant: a lapel microphone, easily hidden behind a buttonhole flower, only costs about £6; a more sophisticated version, no bigger than a sugar-cube, which can be hidden almost anywhere, about £45. Microphones are also commonly built into everyday objects such as ball-point pens, ashtrays, cuff-links and tie-clips etc., prices varying from £12 to £60.

Cameras, another indespensible item of spy equipment, come in a variety of sizes and disguises, the best known being the 16mm Minox with automatic exposure control for about £120; there is also a Russian version which is even smaller in size. The Swiss have produced a small, silent, 35mm motor-driven camera at about £95. Miniaturized tape-recorders and hair-wire recorders which can be hidden easily in the palm of the hand or inserted into signet rings are also available.

In spite of all this highly sophisticated gadgetry now being produced most agents still prefer the age-old techniques of bribery, blackmail and alcohol to loosen tongues for information. They are also much cheaper. The installation of bugs is a risky business for the agent and expensive for the client, especially if the device cannot be recovered later because of its location.

Typical telephone 'bug'. This microphone is usually permanently 'live' once inserted and doubles as the mouthpiece which it replaces.

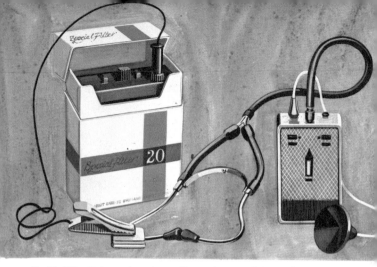

(Left) FM wireless microphone. Battery powered, it has a range of approximately 100 feet. *(Right)* An electronic stethoscope with very high amplification. Used for listening through walls.

At the moment the police can only take very limited action in industrial espionage cases as it is not yet considered an indictable offence. For example, in phone-tapping cases the defendant can only be charged with 'unauthorized interference with GPO equipment and illegal use of GPO electricity'. In the event of an agent being caught on another firm's premises photographing documents, the only possible charges are 'tresspassing' or 'breaking and entering'.

Legitimate business intelligence may sometimes involve the infiltration of an agent into a company, usually achieved by reading the 'appointments vacant' columns, each advertized job presenting a chance to have a spy in the company's midst without anyone ever suspecting his true role. From this 'inside' position he can make an accurate appraisal of the firm, its products and possible areas of future production and expansion. Another method of obtaining the same results is for the agent to advertize himself hiding under the cover of a bogus management consultancy. A lot of information can be gleaned from bogus interviews in such a situation.

The types of firm most likely to receive the attentions of

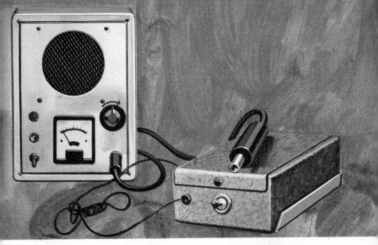

'Deteko' microphone detector. Working on the same principle as a geiger-counter, it indicates by a series of clicks how near the instrument is to a hidden microphone. Earphones or a meter may be used if the search has to be conducted silently. (*Right*) 'Bug' eliminator. Referred to as an 'anti-surveillance unit', it produces a wide band of electronic noise which neutralizes any microphones in the vicinity. Used to counteract the FM type microphone, but is no use against the telephone 'bug' or a wired-up microphone.

industrial spies are those in the toy trade, real estate development, plastics and technological industries such as chemicals, petrochemicals, and electronics, which might also have a military use. In such cases it is sometimes difficult to differentiate between industrial and military espionage.

Clothes and cosmetics must also be added to this list, and even publishing, which has been described on occasions as the most cut and thrust industry of all, relying as it does on creativity and original ideas to sell the product successfully and profitably. In Britain it has been estimated that industry spends something like £1,000 million on research and development for about 26,000 new products a year. All this is the target of the industrial spy and the unscrupulous rival company which uses industrial espionage as a cheap way of obtaining research information and furthering its economic success.

To counteract such activities more and more firms are

relying on the counter-espionage services offered by specialist security firms, a fast-growing and lucrative business. Such firms offer debugging facilities and advice on all kinds of security, but at a price which may be far from cheap. Obvious ways of beating the industrial spy range from the simple exchange of written notes instead of conversation to foil any planted microphones, to the elaborate bug-free room within a room.

The only alternative to hiring the expensive services of a security firm is to organize a department within the company for its exclusive use. In the United States where industrial counter-espionage is already big business, former CIA, NSA and FBI agents are employed as security advisers, while in Great Britain Sir Percy Sillitoe, former Scotland Yard 'gangbuster' and ex-director of DI5, is now the managing director of Security Express and Sir Martin Furnival-Jones, director of DI5 from 1965–72 is the security adviser to ICI.

East v West

The simplest and most direct method of obtaining foreign industrial Intelligence is widely practised at the various International Trade Fairs held in many cities on both sides of the Iron Curtain. A great wealth of information is readily available on such occasions and it is a common sight to see the Russians and their satellite neighbours indiscriminately collecting vast quantities of publicity hand-outs and free samples; literally anything they can lay their hands on legitimately. Needless to say the Western nations indulge in the same kind of activity at the Leipzig and Poznań Trade Fairs, but as always the communists are very security conscious and ensure that nothing of consequence is given away publicly to foreign trade representatives. In the case of the communists collecting Western information it is carried out mainly in order to obtain production details and technical specifications, whereas the Western interest lies in strategic and economic information.

In recent years Soviet Intelligence has concentrated on obtaining information pertaining to electronics, computers and details of items which are not allowed to be exported behind the Iron Curtain. Such information is usually collected

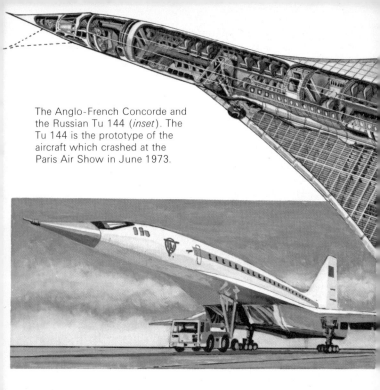

The Anglo-French Concorde and the Russian Tu 144 (*inset*). The Tu 144 is the prototype of the aircraft which crashed at the Paris Air Show in June 1973.

by satellite agents on behalf of the Soviet Union, but directed by East German Intelligence in Berlin.

The most successful of their operations lasted seven years, from 1957 until 1965. Code-named ‚Operation Brunhilde‘ it employed twenty agents to probe the industrial secrets of Great Britain, France and West Germany, culminating in the plans for the Anglo-French Concorde supersonic airliner being passed to Moscow, thus enabling the Russians to build their version and have it in flight first.

The micro-films made by this spy-ring were collected by Jean-Paul Soupert, a retired chemical engineer living in Brussels who had applied for a teaching post in East Germany. The East German Ministry for State Security seized the opportunity to recruit and train him in the basics of espionage and send him home to act as courier and industrial spy. The films

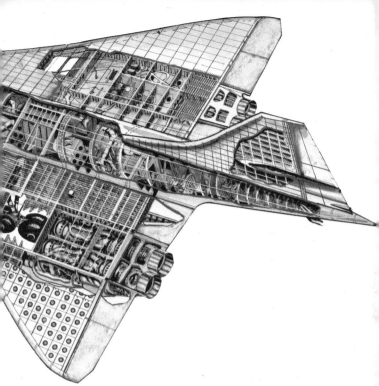

retrieved were then concealed in a variety of objects such as small cigar boxes and tubes of toothpaste which he placed in a toilet on the Ostende-Warsaw express. Agents of the MfS removed the films when the train stopped in East Berlin.

In England the *Brunhilde* agents attempted to penetrate the Kodak photographic laboratories, which were engaged in micro-filming the blueprints for Concorde, and carrying out spectroscopic photography of the aircraft. Two employees of the firm handed over information without ever realizing that it was intended for Moscow.

Soupert in the meantime had been busy in France trying to obtain the French half of the Concorde specifications. In the course of his efforts he aroused the interest of the French DST and Belgian Security who kept him under surveillance and eventually traced several of his contacts to England and

West Germany. The relevant Security Services were informed and by 1964 enough incriminating evidence had been collected to warrant his arrest.

Under interrogation he made a full confession and agreed to co-operate as a double-agent. His fellow-conspirators, however, were scared-off by the arrest and were not convinced by Soupert's reassurances.

The Western Security Services then began a vast counter-espionage action code-named *Operation Air Bubble* against the *Brunhilde* ring. Number One on their wanted list was Herbert Steinbrecher, an East German who had passed to Moscow via the MfS information on chemical processes and details of precision machinery. During the five years that he was active in Western Europe he undertook twenty missions before his arrest by the French DST. A packet of sweets was found in his pocket; upon breaking them open the DST agents found that several contained microfilm of Concorde specifications. The following day British Special Branch detectives arrested the two Kodak employees in London.

Throughout 1965 Western security agents continued to round-up the other members of the *Brunhilde* ring, but it was not until 1967 that a series of trials took place, all held *in camera*. The accused received heavy prison sentences, the longest being given to Peter Kranick, a KGB agent of Polish origin who, it was revealed, was the real head of *Operation Brunhilde*. Steinbrecher received a twelve year sentence.

Three years later, Wolfgang Vogel the spy exchange lawyer arranged for three of the defendants, including Steinbrecher, to be exchanged for three French SDECE agents who were serving prison sentences in East Germany.

As far as the Russians were concerned, *Operation Brunhilde* was a success. It enabled them to build their own version of Concorde, the Tu 144, and have it in the air before the Anglo-French aircraft. It made its first public appearance at the Paris Air Show in 1971 and another modified version was exhibited in June 1973. On the last day of the air show Concorde and then the Tu 144 showed off their paces. In front of 200,000 horrified spectators the Russian aircraft exploded in mid-air and crashed onto a small town north of Paris killing eighteen people.

GLOSSARY

Communist China. Ministry of Public Affairs: Internal Security. Department of Social Affairs: Intelligence/Security Agency. United Front Workers' Department/International Liaison Department: Foreign Intelligence Services.

Egypt. *Muhabbarat El-Amma:* General Intelligence Agency. *Mabahes El-Amma:* Secret Political Police/Internal Security.

France. SDECE: Foreign Intelligence. DST: Internal Security.

East Germany. VfK: Military Intelligence. MfS: Ministry for State Security. HVA: Espionage section of MfS. SSD: State Security Service (Secret Police). K5: former name of the MfS. Administration 19: former name of the VfK.

West Germany. BND: Intelligence Service. BfV: Counter-espionage Service.

Great Britain. DI6: British Intelligence. MI6: former name of British Intelligence. DI5: Security Service. MI5: former name of the Security Service.

Israel. *Mossad:* Intelligence Service. *Sherutei Habitahon (Shin Beth):* Counter-espionage Service.

Poland. Z-2: Military Intelligence. SB: Security Service. UB/*Bezpieka:* former names for the Security Service.

Soviet Union. CHEKA/GPU/OGPU/NKVD/NKGB/MVD/MGB/KGB: various names for the Secret Political Police, in chronological order from 1917 to the present day. GRU: Military Intelligence.

United States. CIA: Central Intelligence Agency. DIA: Defence Intelligence Agency. NSA: National Security Agency. FBI: Federal Bureau of Investigation.

BOOKS TO READ

A History of Modern Espionage by A. Lind, Hodder, 1965.

A History of the British Secret Service by R. Deacon, Muller, 1969.

A History of the Russian Secret Service by R. Deacon, Muller, 1972.

Gehlen: Spy of the Century by E. H. Cookridge, Hodder and Stoughton, 1971.

Industrial Intelligence and Espionage by P. I. Slee Smith, Business Books, 1970.

Network: The Truth about Gen. Gehlen and his Spy Ring by H. Höhne and H. Zolling, Secker and Warburg, 1972.

Private Spies by R. Payne, Barker, 1967.

School for Spies by J. Bernard Hutton, Spearman, 1961.

Spies in the Promised Land by M. Bar-Zohar, Davis-Poynter, 1972.

Spy Trade by E. H. Cookridge, Hodder and Stoughton, 1971.

Struggle in the Dark: How Russian and other Iron Curtain Spies operate by J. Bernard Hutton, Harrap, 1969.

The Codebreakers by D. Kahn, Weidenfeld and Nicholson, 1966.

The Craft of Intelligence by A. Dulles, Weidenfeld, 1963.

The Espionage Establishment by D. Wise and T. B. Ross, Cape, 1968.

The Real CIA by L. B. Kirkpatrick Jr., Macmillan, 1968.

The Russian Secret Police by R. Hingley, Hutchinson, 1970.

The Secret War for Europe by L. Hagen, Macdonald, 1968.

The Super Spies by A. Tully, Arthur Barker, 1970.

Twice Through the Lines by Otto John, Macmillan, 1972.

The Third Man by E. H. Cookridge, Barker, 1968.

INDEX

Page numbers in **bold** type refer to illustrations

SOME OTHER TITLES IN THIS SERIES

■ **Arts**
Antique Furniture/Architecture/Art Nouveau for Collectors/Clocks
and Watches/Glass for Collectors/Jewellery/Musical Instruments/
Porcelain/Pottery/Silver for Collectors/Victoriana

■ **Domestic Animals and Pets**
Budgerigars/Cats/Dog Care/Dogs/Horses and Ponies/Pet Birds/Pets
for Children/Tropical Freshwater Aquaria/Tropical Marine Aquaria

■ **Domestic Science**
Flower Arranging

■ **Gardening**
Chrysanthemums/Garden Flowers/Garden Shrubs/House Plants/
Plants for Small Gardens/Roses

■ **General Information**
Aircraft/Arms and Armour/Coins and Medals/Espionage/Flags/
Fortune Telling/Freshwater Fishing/Guns/Military Uniforms/Motor
Boats and Boating/National Costumes of the world/Orders and
Decorations/Rockets and Missiles/Sailing/Sailing Ships and Sailing
Craft/Sea Fishing/Trains/Veteran and Vintage Cars/Warships

■ **History and Mythology**
Age of Shakespeare/Archaeology/Discovery of: Africa/The American
West/Australia/Japan/North America/South America/Great Land
Battles/Great Naval Battles/Myths and Legends of: Africa/Ancient
Egypt/Ancient Greece/Ancient Rome/India/The South Seas/
Witchcraft and Black Magic

■ **Natural History**
The Animal Kingdom/Animals of Australia and New Zealand/
Animals of Southern Asia/Bird Behaviour/Birds of Prey/Butterflies/
Evolution of Life/Fishes of the world/Fossil Man/A Guide to the
Seashore/Life in the Sea/Mammals of the world/Monkeys and
Apes/Natural History Collecting/The Plant Kingdom/Prehistoric
Animals/Seabirds/Seashells/Snakes of the world/Trees of the
world/Tropical Birds/Wild Cats

■ **Popular Science**
Astronomy/Atomic Energy/Chemistry/Computers at Work/The
Earth/Electricity/Electronics/Exploring the Planets/Heredity/
The Human Body/Mathematics/Microscopes and Microscopic Life/
Physics/Psychology/Undersea Exploration/The Weather Guide